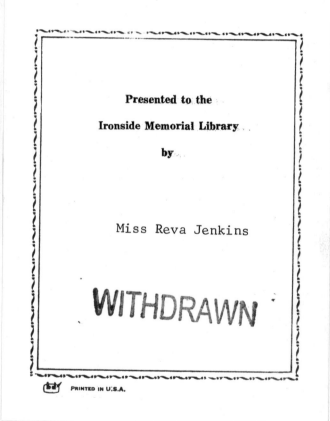

# THE SCHOOL OF NIGHT

*The*

# SCHOOL OF NIGHT

A STUDY IN THE LITERARY
RELATIONSHIPS OF

SIR WALTER RALEGH

*By* M. C. BRADBROOK

*New York*
RUSSELL & RUSSELL
1965

FIRST PUBLISHED IN 1936

REISSUED, 1965, BY RUSSELL & RUSSELL, INC.

BY ARRANGEMENT WITH CAMBRIDGE UNIVERSITY PRESS

L.C. CATALOG CARD NO: 65—18791

PRINTED IN THE UNITED STATES OF AMERICA

To

H. M. R. MURRAY

IN GRATEFUL RECOLLECTION
OF NINE YEARS' TEACHING AND
FRIENDSHIP

# CONTENTS

# PREFACE

The subject of this book seemed to me of interest for two reasons. First, because the connection of Ralegh, Marlowe and Chapman illustrates the critical transition from the early Elizabethan way of writing to the way of Shakespeare and his contemporaries: it shows how the language became complicated with mythology and symbol, and yet flexible with puns and word-play and new verse forms.

Secondly, because it shows the close connection between the development of poetry and the general intellectual life of the age, and the spread of new theories in philosophy and science.

I am indebted in the first place to the Electors to the Allen Scholarship whose award enabled me to write this book, and to Girton College, Cambridge, and Somerville College, Oxford, where I lived in an atmosphere that made writing easy. Miss Jocelyn Otway-Ruthven of Girton College has kindly read the MS. from the point of view of a historian.

The "war" between Shakespeare and the School of Night, which I have dealt with in my last chapter, has been worked out from the complementary point

vii

# PREFACE

of view, in much more detail and with many bio-
graphical sidelights, by Miss Frances M. Yates, in
*A Study of Love's Labour's Lost*, one of the Cambridge
University Press Shakespeare Problems Series. I am
indebted to Miss Yates for permission to see the proofs
of her book: she was also ready to read through my
MS., and make several suggestions.

*March,* 1936                                    M. C. B.

# I

# THE SCHOOL OF NIGHT:
# THE LITERARY RELATIONSHIPS OF
# SIR WALTER RALEGH

## *THE STORY*

Within these woods of Arcadie
He chiefe delight and pleasure tooke,
And on the mountaine Parthenie,
Upon the liquid chrystall brooke,
The Muses met him every day
That taught him sing, to write, and say...

O God, that such a worthy man
In whom so rare desarts did raigne,
Desired thus, must leave us than,
And we to wish for him in vaine!
O could the stars that bred that wit,
In force no longer fixed sit!

MATTHEW ROYDON, *Elegy, or Friend's
Passion, for his Astrophill.*

The relationship of Sir Walter Ralegh to the poets of his time liberally repays investigation, for it was not the usual one of patron and follower: Sir Walter was himself both scholar and poet. He could not be courted in rhyme except indirectly:

To thee, that art the Summer's Nightingale,
Thy sovereign Goddesses most deare delight,
Why do I send this rusticke Madrigale,
That may thy tuneful ears unseason quite?

So wrote Spenser, in sending Ralegh the first three books of *The Faerie Queene*: and Ralegh replied in kind, with one magniloquent and one jesting sonnet,

The prayse of meaner wits this work like profit brings,
As doth the Cuckoes song delight when Philumena sings.

Ralegh could give much more than another patron, not only in stimulative competition, but in breadth of knowledge and general culture, as well as in practical experience of many countries and peoples. His was a shaping influence as well as a provocative one. His own poetry survives only hazardously: it was for the most part occasional verse, and he never published: but its influence can be traced in the writings of Spenser, Marlowe and Chapman. Historically, Ralegh's poetry is of the first importance, and it has seldom had proper appreciation. The literary and historical aspects are in fact so closely related that I

3

propose to give two chapters to an account of Ralegh's literary circle, one to a consideration of his intellectual influence and the reaction against it, and four to the poetry of himself, his friends and his opponents.

To begin with a summary of Ralegh's career. He was born at Hayes Barton, near Budleigh Salterton, about 1552. He came of good Devonshire family: his mother, Katherine Champernoun, was by her first marriage the mother of John, Humphrey and Adrian Gilbert: and besides his famous stepbrothers, Walter Ralegh had an elder brother of the whole blood, Carew. His childhood was spent in Devonshire: some time in his teens he went up to Oriel College, Oxford, and afterwards he was in residence at the Middle Temple. He fought in the French wars of religion under his cousins the Champernouns, and in Ireland under Lord Grey de Wilton: returning thence in 1582 he became, almost at once, one of the most prominent figures at Court.

From 1582 to 1592 he was the reigning favourite of Elizabeth. He was given estates and a monopoly which assured him of a fortune; he was made Lord Warden of the Stanneries, Lord Lieutenant of Cornwall, and Vice-Admiral of the Western Counties. After 1585, as Captain of the Queen's Bodyguard, he might be in daily attendance in the royal apartments. No other man had freer access to Elizabeth's private circle. He was seldom allowed on a campaign or a voyage, or even leave of absence to conduct his own affairs. Nevertheless he financed and directed schemes for the plantation of Ireland and for the colonization of Virginia. In 1589 the arrival at Court of the Earl of Essex and his immediate rise to favour a little clouded the fortunes of Ralegh, who in that year went to Ireland, chased there, it was rumoured, by the new-comer.

But he was soon back. The ten *Bookes of the Ocean's Love to Cynthia* which he had produced in exile helped him to recover Elizabeth's graces. In Ireland he had met Spenser, who describes their friendship in *Colin Clout's Come Home Again.* Ralegh took Spenser back with him to Court, and the first three books of *The Faerie Queene* seem to have formed part of his campaign to recover first place with the Queen.[1]

Things went well till 1592, when Ralegh was recalled from an expedition and after a few weeks clapped into the Tower, ostensibly because he had sailed without leave, actually because of a love affair with Elizabeth Throckmorton, a maid of honour, whom he afterwards married. In the Tower he remained from July to September, and Mistress Throckmorton as well. During this imprisonment he wrote the eleventh *Book of the Ocean's Love to Cynthia*, the only one to survive.

In the autumn his fleet returned with the largest

prize ever brought to England, the Portuguese carrack *Madre de Dios* carrying £150,000 of plunder. The whole country-side was enriched: London was full of talk and ballads on the subject of the Great Carrack. The sailors began looting, and Ralegh was sent to Dartmouth to restore them to order and secure the lion's share of the prize for Elizabeth. After this he lived at Sherborne, his Dorset estate, being forbidden the Court; though he appeared in Parliament as M.P. for St Michael's. He became interested in schemes for the colonization of Guiana: in 1595 he sailed on a voyage of discovery, and he sent another expedition the next year. In 1596 also he played a distinguished part in the attack on Cadiz, when an English fleet raided the harbour and took the town by storm. He was received at Court, and the next year, sailing as Rear-Admiral on the Islands Voyage, he performed the only notable deed of that bungled expedition. He remained at Court till Elizabeth's death, though he never regained his old standing.

Ralegh's life under James may be summed up in few words. The king wanted his removal: in August 1603 he was implicated in the charges of treasonable conspiracy with Spain brought against Lord Cobham. After a brutal and farcical trial, and without a tittle of evidence to convict him, he was sentenced to death: reprieved at the very point of execution, he was then imprisoned for thirteen years, his estates filched from him, his sentence never reversed. In these years he gave himself to the study of chemistry and medicine, and the writing of his *History of the World*. In 1616 James, desperate for money, let Ralegh sail for Guiana in the hopes of discovering a gold-mine. He also betrayed Ralegh's plans to the Spanish ambassador, who passed them on to Madrid. The expedition failed: in a brush with the Spaniards Ralegh's son was killed. Ralegh came home: and to placate the Spaniards James beheaded him in the autumn of 1618 on the charge of 1603.

During the last ten or fifteen years there has been a growing interest in the literary activities of Ralegh, and in particular in the society founded by him, and known now by Shakespeare's nickname "The School of Night".[2] There appears to have been a kind of literary "war" between this school and the faction of Essex, not unlike the dramatists' "war" of 1598–9, or the earlier one between Harvey and Nashe. The idea of the School of Night was first put forward by Arthur Acheson in *Shakespeare and the Rival Poet* (1903), supported by "Q" and Dover Wilson in their edition of *Love's Labour's Lost* (1923), by G. B. Harrison in his edition of *Willobie his Avisa* (1926) and by various writers on Marlowe and Ralegh.

# THE SCHOOL OF NIGHT

Ralegh was the patron of the school; Thomas Harriot, a mathematician of European reputation, was its master. It probably included the earls of Northumberland and Derby, and Sir George Carey, with the poets Marlowe, Chapman, Matthew Roydon and William Warner. They studied theology, philosophy, astronomy, geography and chemistry: and their reputations differed as widely as their studies. Harriot, Marlowe and Ralegh were generally suspected of atheism, if not of direct intercourse with the devil: the earls of Northumberland and Derby were Catholics: Chapman and Roydon were devout Christians, but not of any ascertainable sect.

The three nobles were all of great family and all were eccentrics. Northumberland was known as the Wizard Earl: he was a moody man, interested in alchemy, a patron of the arts, and a scholar. After 1606 he was co-prisoner in the Tower with Ralegh, having been suspected of complicity in the Gunpowder Plot. There he collected a very large library, which included among its few English books Chapman's translation of Homer.

Derby was a poet, an alchemist and also suspected of witchcraft. He too was a patron of poets, and Shakespeare began his career with the company of Lord Strange (as he then was). He died young: it was thought that he had been poisoned: certainly he was very unpopular. His widow married Thomas Egerton: she was the Lady of Milton's *Arcades* and the grandmother of the children who played *Comus*.

George Carey, later Lord Hunsdon and Shakespeare's master from 1596 to 1604, was a man of action. He was first cousin once removed to Elizabeth, and very much in her favour at all times. He held various military posts, and there is a rousing story of how, as Governor of the Isle of Wight, he purged the island of lawyers and quacks, and "in Sir George Carey's time, an attorney coming to settle in the island was, by his command, with a pound of candles hanging at his breech lighted and with bells about his legs, hunted out of the island".

Lady Elizabeth Carey and her daughter, also Elizabeth, were great friends of the poets and in particular of Edmund Spenser and Thomas Nashe.

These gentlemen, and the poets, whose lives are read sometimes with more interest than their poetry, were instructed by Thomas Harriot, from whose work Descartes himself is reputed to have learned. His discoveries in algebra and in pure mathematics generally were his greatest achievement, though his refusal to publish made it possible for others to gain reputations which should have been his. Some of his papers were collected in the eighteenth century by an industrious German antiquary.[3] He is said to have been ahead of Galileo in his use of the telescope: certainly he observed Halley's comet in 1609 very precisely. He kept up a correspondence with Kepler and other continental scientists, and worked steadily at astronomy and the allied studies of optics and transmission of light.

Ralegh had taken Harriot into his house as mathematical tutor as early, probably, as 1580. In 1585 he went to Virginia with Ralegh's expedition and stayed a year, returning with the rest of the first settlement in Drake's fleet. In 1588 he published *A Brief and True Report of the Newfound Land of Virginia*. In this survey the crops, merchandise, fauna and mineral wealth of the country are set forth in a remarkably crisp and scientific way. Nothing comparable to it in systematic method or precision was produced by an Elizabethan explorer.

It was probably about this time that Ralegh introduced Harriot to Northumberland, with whom he had recently become friendly. The earl took to Harriot: in 1597 he granted him a pension, and Harriot with Walter Warner and Robert Hughes were known as the Earl's Three Magi.

But Harriot also remained faithful to Ralegh. During the years of their imprisonment he transacted business for both his patrons: he helped Ralegh to collect material for his *History of the World* and there is evidence that he was with him on the night before his execution. The Earl of Northumberland gave Harriot residence at Sion House, Isleworth, where he lived from 1607 till his death in 1621, earning his living apparently by making telescopes. In his will he left to the earl "my two perspective trunckes wherein I use espetially to see Venus horned like the Moone and the Spottes in the Sun...".

The minor mathematicians and poets who filled up the circle, the two Warners, Hughes, perhaps Edward Blunt, call for little attention. The most interesting of the lesser men is Matthew Roydon. He was a leading literary figure of the eighties, described by Nashe as the author of "many most absolute comicke inventions (made more publicke by every man's praise then they can bee by my speech)". His only considerable work to survive is the *Elegy or Friends Passion for His Astrophill*, printed with Spenser's collection of elegies on Philip Sidney, but his reputation is suggested by the tone of deference in which Chapman writes, dedicating his first two poems to Roydon, and by the righteous indignation with which Kyd couples him with the "atheist" Marlowe.

Such were the members of the group which included also Marlowe and Chapman, the "schola frequens de atheismo" of which the Jesuit Parsons wrote in 1592.[4] In the English version of his pamphlet he speaks of

Sir Walter Rawley's school of Atheisme by the way, and of the Conjuror that is M(aster) thereof, and of the diligence used to get young gentlemen of this school, wherein both Moyses and our Saviour, the olde and the Newe Testamentes are jested at, and the scollers taught, among other things, to spell God backwards.

Sir Walter's school had much wider interests than those credited to it by such scandalized outsiders. It was both more serious and less serious than their reports would imply. Nevertheless the different rumours have such uniformity as to give a reasonable picture of the way in which the members of the school behaved in public.

For example, Parsons' words about Harriot confirm Antony à Wood's account of him: and Aubrey mentions the anagram: "I remember my first Ld Scudamour sayd, 'Twas basely sayd of Sir W. R. to talk of the anagram of dog'."

The informer Richard Baines, bringing charges of atheism against one Richard Cholmley in 1593, said:

He sayeth and verily believeth that one Marlowe is able to show more sound reasons for Atheisme, than any divine in England is able to give to prove divinitie, and that Marloe told him that he hath read the Atheist lecture to Sir Walter Raleigh and others.

# THE STORY

This is the clearest external evidence of the connection between Marlowe and Ralegh: Kyd mentioned that the poet conversed with "Harriot, Warner, Roydon and some stationers in Paul's churchyard" and also that he meant to go to Scotland "whither I hear Roydon is gone and where if he had lived he told me when I saw him last he meant to be".[5] Baines also mentioned Harriot.

It was in consequence of Kyd's statements that Marlowe was summoned to appear before the Privy Council on May 18th, 1593. He does not appear to have been in any great danger, before the brawl at Deptford in which he was killed on May 30th. It has been suggested that this fray was planned by Sir Walter Ralegh and the School of Night to stop Marlowe's mouth; but there is not, I think, any convincing evidence for the view.[6]

Next March a commission sat at Cerne Abbas, Dorset, to enquire into the rumours of a set of atheists there: it was obviously directed at Sir Walter Ralegh, who was living at Sherborne close by. The local clergy had nearly all heard rumours of the atheism of Ralegh and Harriot: they were said "to have brought the Godhead in question and the whole course of the Scriptures", and Harriot, it was thought, had been cited before the Privy Council for denying the resurrection of the body. But only one man could produce

13

more than hearsay evidence: and the enquiry was not followed up.

The conclusion to be drawn from the testimony of Kyd, Baines and the Devonshire clergy is that the school did not disclose its opinions to the generality: that it enjoyed scandalizing the godly and confounding the dogmatic; that it was provocative and irreverent, out of deliberate policy or natural devilment or both.

It was only their attitude towards historic Christianity which concerned the general public; and here Ralegh showed himself the very antithesis of the credulous traveller who reported a race of headless men in South America. He examined the facts of Scripture in a spirit rather akin to that of the Modern Churchmen. If Harriot's scientific experiments suggested a naturalistic explanation of the miracles and a repudiation of the Book of Genesis, they might still leave untouched the foundations of Christian metaphysics. But this was a distinction which few people would be able to make at the time. The Reformation was not yet old enough for the difference between Christendom and Christianity to be plain. Though there were now more churches than one, there was no mutual recognition or toleration between them. Marlowe and Ralegh both emphasized the separation between Christian doctrine and organized Christianity, the one in *Tamburlaine Part II* and *The Jew of Malta*, the other in *The Lie* and *The Passionate Man's Pilgrimage*.

Public tradition records only an attack upon the literal interpretation of the Bible, conducted with more spirit than propriety. In the prose of Ralegh and the poetry of the rest, there is a less direct but more reliable suggestion of an attempt to relate Christian beliefs to the philosophy of the ancients, and to explore the problems of epistemology. The serious work of the School of Night can only be deduced from the writings of the members, and then incompletely.

It is therefore proposed to consider first the accounts of its religious beliefs which are the work of outsiders, and secondly the writings of the school.

Harriot, Ralegh and Marlowe are the only members whose "atheism" was a public scandal. Their speeches, as reported by their contemporaries, are very different from their writings and quite incompatible with the Christian fervour of Roydon and Chapman.

Unfortunately no accounts of Harriot's conversation survive, for, although considered the most diabolical of the three, he was too much of a recluse to give much food for public gossip.

Ralegh and Marlowe had each a keen tongue and a malicious liveliness of temper: but it may also have seemed to them that a sharp jest was more convincing to the average man than a long oration. They tilted against the letter of Christian dogma, exposing contradictions in the Scriptures, producing natural (and often scandalous) explanations of the miracles or making obscene jokes about "Moyses and our Saviour". Their tone is very belligerent; evidently the school chafed against the current attitude which gave divine inspiration to the literal meaning of Scripture and forbade any questioning by the reason. To restrict intelligent enquiry by a set of unsupported assumptions was to Marlowe and Ralegh the unforgivable sin:

> I count religion but a childish toy,
> And hold there is no sin but ignorance.

On the other hand their attempts to question the Shibboleths of the multitude roused a blind hatred and rage. In the popular ballads Ralegh was classed with a figure who often symbolized Satan himself:

> Damnable fiend of hell,
> Mischievous *Machiavel*.

Nothing could better show the need of Marlowe and Ralegh than the hysteric quality of the counter-attacks. Marlowe seems only to have been stirred to higher flights, but Ralegh, an older and more diplomatic character, fell back on indirect methods. Marlowe would "jest at the Scriptures, gybe at prayers, and strive in arguments to frustrate and confute what hath been spoken or wryte by prophets or such holy men".[7] He also suggested administering the Sacrament in a pipe of the devil's weed, tobacco, offered to rewrite the New Testament in better Greek, and so forth. But among these squibs and crackers there are traces of a propagandist intent:

That the first beginning of religion was only to keep men in awe.... He persuades men to atheism, willing them not to be afeard of bugbears and hobgoblins.[8]

These remarks he would "sodenlie take slight occasion to slyp out" in his ordinary conversation. Kyd and Baines were both uneducated and could not distinguish between a joke and an argument; in their reports they mix up all the things which struck their commonplace minds as scandalous. They never produce any of Marlowe's "sound reasons" for atheism, only the flash and smoke of his wit. Indeed, they interlard blasphemy with sedition, charging him with wishing to coin money and with Scottish intrigue. Both sound enraged as well as scandalized; for the poet could not have suffered fools gladly, and his habit of sharpening his dagger on their heads may have an outward and visible sign of his conversational practice. Baines' note concludes:

He saieth likewise that he hath quoted a number of Contrarieties out of the Scripture which he hath given to some great men who in convenient time shall be named.

One of the great men provides a clue in his own writings:

To believe what all men say of the same thing is not possible: for then we shall believe Contrarieties: for some men say that that very thing is pleasant, which others say is displeasant. If it be said we must believe only some men, let it be showed who those men are: for the Platonists will believe Plato, but the Epicures Epicurus, the Pythagoreans Pythagoras, and other philosophers the masters of their own sects: so that it is doubtful to which of them all we shall give credit.[9]

There can be little doubt that it was in this spirit that Ralegh approached the Scriptures, and that therefore his scepticism was not specifically anti-religious, but part of his general philosophic attitude.

The Raleghs were of a temper like to Marlowe's and their birth authorized haughtiness. One of the clergy-men who gave evidence before the commission at Cerne Abbas was still, after three years, smarting under the memory of a gibe. Nicholas Jeffrey,

about some three yeres past cominge to Blandford out of Hampshire, his horse was stayed and taken for a post horse by Sir Walter Rawlegh and Mr Carewe Ralegh: where this deponent entreatinge to have his horse released for that he was to ride home unto his charge (from whence he had been some tyme absent)

to preache the nexte daye beinge sundaye, whereunto
Mr Carewe Raleigh replyed, that he this deponent
might go home when he woulde: but his horse should
preach before him; or to that effect.

His brother appears on this occasion to have kept
quiet: and Dorset had not heard of the anagram of dog.

In this enquiry the Raleghs seem to be associated
in the public mind with their follower Thomas Allen,
Lieutenant of Portsmouth Castle, and with his servant
Oliver, who were swaggering blades and little more.
Allen tore out leaves from the Bible to dry tobacco on,
and cursed God for sending rain to spoil his hawking
party. Oliver was likeminded. In a walk home with
two female friends from divine service, one of the latter
praised the parson's discourse, and Oliver sourly
replied that he might have made it shorter. Mistress
Whetcomb properly if illogically replied to that, that
if you love the Word of God you cannot be weary of
hearing it. Whereupon Oliver, becoming more asser-
tive, said that he believed in Jesus Christ and that
Jesus Christ was a god: but if a man believe all in the
Scriptures he must believe that Moses had fifty-two
whores.

"Whores?" said Mistress Whetcomb.
"Nay, concubines", said he.

Whereupon Mistress Brewer said it was Solomon
he meant, and so bade him go home to sleep "for"

(as Mistress Brewer firmly adds) "she did well per-
ceave he was gone with drink".

Like Kyd and Baines, Dorset was too scandalized
to distinguish between a drunken servant's bit of
bawdry and Sir Walter's adroit shafts. When the Rev.
Ralph Ironside reports the after-dinner conversation
at Sir George Trenchard's, it is evident that Ralegh
is manœuvring the discourse. He begins with a
Socratic pretence of ignorance, fillips the parson's
pride, waits for the expected move, counters it, and,
when he is bored with the game, stops it all with a
single tactful if ironic remark. Falstaff in Shallow's
orchard was not more in command of what passed
over the pippins and carraways.

Carew Ralegh had provoked the discussion with
some "loose speeches" and Sir George Trenchard had
pulled him up: then Sir Walter, returning to a dropped
question, started a dispute on the reasonable soul. He
asked the parson for a definition, saying that though
he was an Oxford man and had disputed in the schools,
"hitherto in this poynt have I not by any been
resolved". The parson promptly pattered off "Aristotle 2º de Anima cap. 1º" but Sir Walter absolutely
rejected Aristotle as "obscure and intricate".

Mr Ironside, a little more heatedly, we may suppose,
said that the soul was "a spiritual and immortal
substance breathed into man by God".

# THE STORY

"Yea, but what is that spiritual and immortal substance?" saith Sir Walter.

"The soul", quoth I.

"Nay, then," said he, "you reason not like a scholar."

Mr Ironside valiantly asserted that arguments about first principles must necessarily proceed in circles. Sir Walter retorted that mathematical principles could be proved by demonstration: as, that "totus est minus quamlibet sua parte: and aske me of it, I can shew it, in the table, in the window, in a man". Mr Ironside replied that this showed *quod est*, not *quid est*: and that demonstration was possible to the senses, but not to the soul, which proceeded from God.

"Marry," quoth Sir Walter, "these two be like: for neither could I learn hitherto what God is."

A Mr Fitzjames gave Aristotle's definition, "Ens Entium", and thus reinforced Mr Ironside said divinity wanted not Aristotle to support it: God *was* Ens Entium, whatever Aristotle chose to say.

"It was most certain, and confirmed by God Himself unto Moyses."

"Yea," said Sir Walter (in his Devonshire drawl), "but what is Ens Entium?"

I answered, "It is God". And being misliked as before, Sir Walter wished that grace might be sayd: "for that", quoth he, "is better than this disputaccion."

21

# THE SCHOOL OF NIGHT

How much bitterness the comparative might cover was not revealed to Mr Ironside.

"He was a bold man and would venture at a discourse, which was displeasing to the Churchmen",[10] as it was meant to be. Ralegh's disdain for the average man led him, though not so plainly as it led Marlowe, to hold argument in leash and let wit run free. If he were among his equals he could be impressive, as Sir John Harington reports in *Nugae Antiquae*:

In religion he hath shown in private talk great depth and good reading, as I once experienced at his own house before many learned men.

Whilst the general public looked on the School of Night with horror, and rejoiced in Marlowe's death as an example to the atheists, the more critical minds were amused by its esoteric profundities, and sceptical of its tacit claims. *Love's Labour's Lost* is not the riposte of the man in the street. The scandalous and "atheistic" aspect of the school is completely ignored, and it is attacked on the score of behaviour, not beliefs. Shakespeare had of course only heard of the doctrine from outside, and *Love's Labour's Lost* is not an answer in the sense of being a refutation. It takes the line, which would prove fatal to most schools of philosophy, of pointing out that the practices of the philosophers do not square with their theory. Strategically it is a

# THE STORY

good piece of outflanking, and the School of Night could not meet it by further ridicule, but only, in *Willobie his Avisa*, with the heavy guns of morality.

The literary warfare between the School of Night and Essex' group belongs to the years 1593–5. In fact it sprang up as soon as the school became really notorious through the disgrace of Ralegh and the death of Marlowe. It is difficult to say how long it had been in existence before this time, but it is not likely to have been older than 1585. Ralegh was absorbed in the expedition to Virginia before that year, and Harriot was away with the colonists. There was probably a break in 1589, the year of Ralegh's Irish trip: the visit of Spenser may have stimulated his interest in poetry. At all events, after his imprisonment he took up his studies with new enthusiasm. In 1593 rumours began to mention atheism. Ralegh was by that time at liberty and divided his time between Sherborne and London. On May 30th Marlowe was killed: next March, the enquiry was held at Cerne Abbas. After that, things blew over, and Ralegh's attention turned towards Guiana. He sent Captain Whiddon to reconnoitre, and set sail himself in 1595.

But the members of the school continued in friendship, and their literary connections can be traced all through the nineties. The active literary war belongs to the years 1593–5. Early in 1593 Chapman wrote *The Shadow of Night*: Shakespeare, the poet of the rival camp, somehow contrived to see it in manuscript, and parodied both the poem and the movement in *Love's Labour's Lost*, produced in the winter season of 1593–4. Chapman then rewrote parts of his poem, which had been intended to help Ralegh in his campaign to recover the favour of Elizabeth, and published the poem *after* the play had appeared, hoping to discredit the attack by a thundering preface addressed to Matthew Roydon. The school collaborated to produce a retort, and *Willobie his Avisa* was entered for publication in September 1594, mocking Essex and Southampton and the latest product of their poet, *The Rape of Lucrece*. Nashe had been, as usual, alive to the fight, and in October he produced a very two-edged pamphlet entitled *The Terrors of the Night*, written apparently while he was staying with the Careys in the Isle of Wight. In 1595 Chapman rather belatedly brought out his *Ovid's Banquet of Sense*, another attempt to beat Shakespeare in narrative poetry, and with another belligerent preface to Roydon. This concluded the literary war.

In 1596 Ralegh's friend and follower, Captain Lawrence Keymis, returned from the second voyage to Guiana, and published an account of it. Chapman wrote a prefatory poem, *De Guiana Carmen Epicum*, in which he glorified the enterprise and its author Ralegh.

But Ralegh was no longer interested in poems, and Chapman was poor; he had to look elsewhere for patronage. In 1598 he published a fragment of his translation of the *Iliad, Achilles' Shield,* dedicated to the Earl of Essex. Nevertheless, there is also a long introductory poem, addressed "To his admired and soul-loved friend, master of all essential and true knowledge, Mr Harriots". In this Chapman bitterly laments his poverty and the shifts to which it drives him, and it constitutes another private dedication, a repudiation of the first. In the preface to the complete translation, Chapman declares that Harriot and Robert Hughes are the only two people who have seen and commented on the work, and concludes a long description of their virtues, "Which two, I protest, are all, and preferred to all".

In the same year (1598) he published his continuation of *Hero and Leander,* a proof of the depths of his friendship for Marlowe: for Chapman believed too firmly in the sacred character of the poet to undertake a work of this kind except from strong personal motives. The same factor applies to all his dedications, for he was remarkably independent: the preface to his lament for Prince Henry, addressed to a poor friend, is perhaps the strongest proof of his disinterestedness.

# THE SCHOOL OF NIGHT

In 1600 Marlowe's song, *The Passionate Shepherd to his Love*, and Ralegh's answer to it, probably written in Marlowe's lifetime, appeared together in *England's Helicon*. (They had been published in a mutilated form a year before in *The Passionate Pilgrim*.)

Such is the external history of the School of Night. A detailed examination of the poetry may show something more.

# II

# THE SCHOOL OF NIGHT

## *THE MEN*

Old John Long, who then wayted on Sir W. Long, being one tyme in the privy garden, with his master, saw the earle of Nottingham wipe the dust from Sir Walter R.'s shoes with his cloake, in compliment....

AUBREY's Brief Lives, II, p. 184.

Sir Walter arrived with his keeper Mr Blount. I assure you, sir, his poor servants, to the number of a hundred and forty goodly men, and all the mariners, came to him with such shouts of joy as I never saw a man more troubled to quiet them in my life.

ROBERT CECIL to THOMAS HENEAGE, Sept. 1592.

Ralegh is easily the most distinguished writer of the Court of Elizabeth. He was a generous patron of the arts and sciences, and the friend of many poets. Spenser seems to have been more intimate with him than with anyone else at the Court: Marlowe knew him: Chapman was in his circle: and Jonson was tutor to his son. Many scholars helped him to collect the material for his *History of the World*.

His works cover a period reaching from Gascoigne and Turberville to the death of Shakespeare. During Elizabeth's reign he was ranked among the first love poets: Puttenham, Meres and Gabriel Harvey mention him as deservedly famous. Later his *History of the World* shadowed his reputation as a poet: and in his imprisonment he wrote less poetry. The *History* was meant to interest James, who condemned it as "too saucy in censuring the acts of kings". Prince Henry appreciated poetry, but he had plenty of other poets: and though he is supposed to have said of Ralegh "Only my father could keep such a bird in a cage", it was easier to hold his attention with treatises on ship-building, and models of ships. Ralegh as a poet belongs to the sixteenth century and to the Court of Elizabeth.

The atmosphere of that Court was wonderfully congenial to one half of him. His taste for a public rôle was as strong as the queen's: his wit was of the same turn, quick and dangerous but not spiteful: he was at home on ceremonial occasions, and in gorgeous clothes: he could outplay most men as the court gallant. He combined such agreeable qualities with the shrewdness and ability in administration which made (for instance) his Wardenship of the Stanneries such a success. During the unloading of the Great Carrack, Cecil testified to "his busyness,...in which he can toil terribly". His soldiership was not theoretic: it had been tested by ten years' experience: his seamanship was comprehensive enough to include shipbuilding and gunnery, as well as navigation and strategy. He was distinguished from noblemen like Leicester and Essex by his practical experience and power of administration: and they never considered him quite of their class, though his family had a longer and more honourable history than either the Dudleys or the Devereux.

The arts of a courtier were dress, wit and social accomplishments, the power to spin out of himself sufficient vivacity to hold the attention of as brilliant and insatiable a mind as Queen Elizabeth's. The pomp and ritual of her Court were no matters of necessity or habit: splendid settings and ceremonious ostentation were an appetite in her. Actions which seem flamboyant and theatrical were inevitable in that world. Ralegh could rise to them naturally: he did not have to make himself taller by standing on tiptoe.

THE MEN

The story of the cloak may be apocryphal, but it is characteristic. His court poetry was part of the ritual; and it was unlaboured, which gave it the more grace. Poetry was an opportunity to combine wit and the Pride of Life: Elizabeth demanded both. The atmosphere in which it was written was competitive, taut and lively: cut-throat jests and desperate compliments flew: a fortune or a reputation might be made and lost overnight. Money matters were disguised like pills in comfits, but everyone from Elizabeth downwards was short of money, and the scramble for office was not a gentlemanly game.

Ralegh had presence and *panache*; his wit was biting, his "honour flashed off exploit". His irony (that weapon of wit employed in the service of pride) antagonized many at Court: but his pride itself was proverbial. "He was a tall, handsome, and bold man: but his naeve was, he was damnable proud." So Aubrey. London made ballads on him:

> Ralegh doth time bestride,
> He sits 'twixt wind and tide,
> Yet uphill he cannot ride,
> For all his bloody pride....
>
> He seeks taxes in the tin,
> He polls the poor to the skin,
> Yet he vows 'tis no sin,
> Lord for thy pity!

The other favourite adjective for him was "bold". It applied to his outward bearings and his social habits. When he was yet a student of the Middle Temple, a friend wrote an anagram which afterwards grew very popular:

The foe to the stomacke and the word of disgrace
Shows the name of the gentleman with the bold face.[1]

For Ralegh did not confine his assertion of superiority to his enemies, or restrict it to "the bitter bob".

In his youth his companions were boisterous blades, but generally those that had wit...one (was) Charles Chester...a perpetual talker, made a noyse like a drum in a room, so one time at a tavern Sir W. R. beates him and seales up his mouth, his upper and neather beard, with hard wax.[2]

It was the more galling that one of such rashness should not give his enemies an opening by quarrelling in the Court, as Essex was to do. In his youth Ralegh had been several times jailed for brawling: but he did not persist in the habit. Yet in 1597, at the age of 45, he could rival Essex in sporting enthusiasm at the attack on Cadiz. Essex "cast his hat into the sea for joy" when Ralegh at the harbour called out "Entramos", but it was Ralegh who sailed into action answering the guns of the fort with scornful blares of the trumpet, and who swung his ship athwart the channel that none of the other English commanders might take the lead of him that day.

Yet Ralegh himself was never "a boisterous blade". It is difficult to realize how he combined the mood of "Cadiz Action" with a disinterested taste for philosophy and science; a nearly disinterested taste for colonization; the capacity to write a *History of the World* and "a vein" for "dittie and amorous ode... most loftie, insolent and passionate".[3]

The queen's intimates underlined their exclusiveness, and organized the supply of compliments (which had to be maintained at all costs) by private names, symbols and tokens. Their minds naturally ran on such lines: heraldry was still a science, allegory was still a mainspring of the arts: the "languages" of flowers, colours and jewels were instruments of social intercourse. Insignia were as yet more than merely decorative, and the offices of the Great Household more than nominal. The delicate games of tokens and poetry were essential to a world where personal relationships were never merely private, and where public relationships were never merely formal. If they gave dignity to the one, they gave grace to the other; and the like could not be found nowadays, except perhaps in the Far East.

So Sir Thomas Heneage, "in the cold north country where no butterflies were", received from the queen a mother-of-pearl butterfly as a token: and Ralegh's half-brother Humphrey Gilbert, when about to start on a voyage, had "a figure of an anchor guided by a lady".

The exchange of tokens is recalled in *The Book of the Ocean's Love to Cynthia*:

> The tokens hung on breast and kindly worn,
> Are now elsewhere disposed or held for toys.
>
> (ll. 263–4.)

The fashionable pastoralism was adopted by the inner circle: Elizabeth was known as Cynthia or the Shepherdess.[4] Her private name for Ralegh was Water, an obvious pun on his Christian name and his profession.

On one occasion Sir Christopher Hatton, being jealous of Ralegh, sent Elizabeth a reproachful letter and some tokens, among them a small bucket to signify "Water".

She sent a verbal answer, "that if Princes were like Gods (as they should be) they would suffer no element so to abound as to breed confusion", and for better assurance that he should fear no drowning, she sent him a bird, a dove, "that together with the rainbow brought the good tidings and the covenant that there should be no more destruction by water".[5]

Ralegh adopted this name for his poetry. He called himself the Ocean; Spenser, the Shepherd of the

Ocean; suggesting the magnetic control of Cynthia, who swayed him as the moon sways the tide. But if need was, he could use his poetry as an instrument of intrigue as readily as Hatton had used the tokens: it was a weapon in his hand. In July 1587 the Earl of Essex wrote to Sir Edward Dyer describing a scene in which he had behaved with his customary violence. The queen had snubbed his sister, and Essex took it that she had done so at Ralegh's instigation. He burst out into abuse in the presence of Ralegh himself, who was on duty as Captain of the Bodyguard. The queen refused to take any notice of him: and in a fit of rage he took horse and rode off from the Court. He said to Dyer:

She came to speak of Ralegh and it seemed she could not well endure anything to be spoken against him: and taking hold of one word (Disdain) she said there was no cause why I should disdain him. This speech disturbed me so much that as near as I could I did describe unto her what he had been and what he was: and then I did let her see whether I had cause to disdain his competition of Love: or whether I could have comfort to give myself over to the service of a Mistress that was in Awe of such a man. I spake what of grief and choler as much against him as I could: and I think he standing at the door might very well hear the worst that I spoke of him....She made no answer but turned her away to my lady of Warwick.[6]

# THE SCHOOL OF NIGHT

A scrap of paper in Ralegh's writing survives among the Cecil papers at Hatfield. It is generally voted "a riddle" and has so far baffled all editors and commentators. But it fits so neatly into Essex' letter that that document may reasonably be looked on, I think, as the other half of the riddle. The poem runs:

If Cynthia be a Queen, a princess and supream,
Keip these among the rest, or say it was a dreame.
For those that like, expound, and those that loath,
  express
Meanings according as their minds are moved more
  or less.
For writing *what thou art or showing what thou were*
Adds to the one *dysdayne*, to th' other but *despair*.
Thy mind of neyther needs, in both seeing it exceeds.

Ralegh at his post could not reply: nor could he challenge Essex, as he was to do later, for officially he had not heard what was said. Therefore this curt little verse was probably "put into a pocket", like the love poem to Lady Laiton. It may be paraphrased:

As Cynthia is a queen, a princess and supreme (or by Cynthia who is...), pocket up these verses with the rest of your choler or imagine you only dreamt of their arrival. For those people who are friendly and popular (like = enjoy and prove enjoyable) state a case, and those who are unfriendly and unpopular pour out what is in their minds: how much they say depends on how much they are moved (i.e. I am not moved by

36

your rage and therefore I say little). To write what you now are or what you were on that evening would make the former kind of people (i.e. myself) only disdainful and the latter kind (i.e. you) only despairing. And your mind has no need of either quality, seeing that you already exceed in both.

As a piece of well-adjusted contempt it could hardly be bettered. The repetition of Essex' own phrases, the even superciliousness of the balanced clauses, and the snap of the final line are a matter of technical control: Ralegh is opposing the "grief and choler" of the young nobleman who had jeered at his family with something more disconcerting than rage.

This poem may be taken as typical of his better early works, which were at their worst merely rhetorical exercises upon the "figures" (e.g. *Your face, your tongue, your wit*) with no more than a cerebral stimulant behind them. This poem is written in a mood of tension: the hard dentals, *ds* and *ts*, set the reader's jaw. It reflects only the immediate mood, but it does so very adequately. It is perhaps too thoroughly occasional verse to compare with poetry of the same date which he addresses directly to Elizabeth (*Praisd be Diana's Fair and Harmless Light*).

But the Court and court poetry did not absorb all Ralegh's time or his interests. His interest in scholarship led him to join or to found several learned societies.

He was a member of Archbishop Parker's Society of Antiquaries, the forerunner of the Royal Society. This society met every week for discussion: Camden and Selden were members also, and here Ralegh formed friendships which were to stand him in good stead when he undertook the *History of the World*. He is said to have founded Ben Jonson's club at the Mermaid as well.

Ralegh was an eager reader: according to Aubrey he used to take a trunkful of books to sea with him, where he could study undisturbed. He read French and Spanish fluently, as well as the learned tongues: but he had no Hebrew.

History, philosophy and theology seem to have been his chief interests. Mathematics and geography were included, probably in connection with navigation. He was famous as a chemist, and engaged in the search for an Elixir of Life. His cordial, which in 1613 restored Prince Henry to a last flicker of consciousness, may have been compounded of quinine: during his voyages of discovery he noted with care the medical remedies of the natives.

In all these studies, in all the more scholarly side of his life, Ralegh would be able to count upon Harriot. It was a friendship which was not without risk, for Harriot's suspected traffic with the devil fitted in with the popular picture of Ralegh the Mischievous

Machiavel. When the latter was condemned to death in 1603, the judge in passing sentence flung at him his association with "that devil Harriot", as one of his notorious crimes.

Antony à Wood accuses Harriot of Deism, and goes on to say:

He had strange thoughts of the Scriptures, and always undervalued the old story of the creation of the world. . . . He made a *Philosophical Theology* wherein he cast off the Old Testament, so that consequently the New would have no foundation. . . .

It is probable that Harriot was intellectually the backbone of the School of Night. He may also have been responsible for the "enticing" of the young gentlemen of which Parsons speaks, for he was mathematical tutor to many youths of distinguished family: among others, Robert Sidney, Sir Philip's "sweet Robyn".

There is no direct evidence for Harriot being irreligious. When in Virginia, he read the Bible to the Indians with fervour; and in 1616, under the pain of cancer of the lips, he wrote to his physician:

I believe in God Almighty, I believe that medicine was ordained by Him; I trust the physician as His minister. My faith is sure, my hope is firm. I wait however with patience for everything in its own time according to His providence. We must act earnestly, fight boldly, but in His name, and we shall conquer.

Another member of the school was Lawrence Keymis, a scholar and a sailor. He had been made a Fellow of Balliol in 1583: later he became Notary and Bursar, and remained a Fellow till 1591. He was skilled in geography and mathematics to a fair degree: he could turn a neat Latin verse and must have been a man of general culture. In 1595 he accompanied Ralegh on a voyage to Guiana: he led the expedition of 1596, and wrote an account of it when he returned. For the rest of his life Captain Keymis devoted himself to the service of Ralegh. He was imprisoned for him in 1603: this emerges in one of the bypasses during Ralegh's trial.

*Ralegh.* This poor man (Keymis) hath been close prisoner these eighteen weeks. He was offered the rack to make him confess.

*Lord Henry Howard.* No circumstance moveth me more than this: Keymishe was never at the rack. The King gave charge that no rigour should be used.

*The other commissioners.* We protest before God, there was no such matter to our knowledge.

*Ralegh.* Was not the keeper of the rack sent for: and he threatened with it?

# THE MEN

*Sir William Waad.* When Mr Solicitor and myself came to examine Keymishe we told him "he deserved the rack" but did not threaten him with it.

*The other commissioners.* It was more than we knew.

During the years in the Tower, Keymis, like Harriot, acted as Ralegh's agent: he advised Lady Ralegh about the management of the estates, and became one of the trustees for Sherborne. It was chiefly on his information that the last expedition to Guiana was undertaken: and when Ralegh fell sick on the coast, he led the expedition up-country in which young Ralegh was killed. Ralegh, recounting his story in the *Apology*, adds, "After my son was slain, I knew he had no care at all of any man surviving". Keymis did not reach the mine (partly because, thinking Sir Walter had also died of his sickness, he no longer felt any motive for thrusting through the Spaniards), and he returned to a stormy interview with his friend and master:

I told him he had undone me by his obstinacy and that I could not favour or colour in any sort his former folly. He then asked me, whether that were my resolution: I answered that it was: he then replied in these words: "I know then, sir, what course to take": and went out of my cabin into his own, in which he was no sooner entered than I heard a pistol go off. I sent up (not suspecting any such thing as the killing of himself) to know who shot a pistol: Keymis himself made answer, lying on his bed, that he had shot it off because it had been long charged: with which I was satisfied. Some half hour after this his boy going into his cabin found him dead, having a long knife thrust under his left pap through the heart, and his pistol lying by him, with which it appeared that he had shot himself: but the bullet lighting upon a rib, had but broken the rib, and went no further.... Now he that knew Keymis, did also know that he was of that obstinate resolution, and a man so far from caring to please or satisfy any man but myself, as no man's opinion, from the greatest to the least, could have persuaded him to have laid violent hands on himself....[7]

Keymis is a typical figure, in that he represents the attitude of all Ralegh's immediate followers. In public he was hated, but the personal servants and the sailors whom he commanded were always loyal to him. At his execution he remembered a cook who had been accused of poisoning him, but who, having once been his servant, he was sure would go a thousand miles to do him good. Ralegh's relations with Keymis are as significant in their personal implications as those with Harriot. Such were the men who gathered in Ralegh's house for discussion: there were also Marlowe, poet and government agent; Chapman, poet and recluse; and perhaps "the first poet of the age" who was no recluse, though exiled.

# THE MEN

The connection of Spenser with Ralegh's circle must remain conjectural; but if he were in contact with Marlowe some time in the eighties, it would explain how Marlowe came to see a manuscript of *The Faerie Queene* before writing *Tamburlaine Part II*, and so to borrow the passage about the almond tree. Certainly Spenser's philosophic ideas have a great resemblance to those of the school.

The obvious thing about the group of noblemen, scholars and petty officials is the versatility of each of the members. They were nearly all men of genuinely practical interests: but also scholars and poets. Their capacity for digesting the most different forms of experience is astonishing. Nobles were usually anxious to live at Court, and that provided a full-time occupation, while the poets were all preoccupied with earning their living and keeping out of the Fleet. Ralegh's passion for argument and for exploring other minds was the centripetal power.

Ralegh was not only intellectually but temperamentally a myriad-minded man. He seems at first sight only self-contradictory: he could be generous or ferocious beyond most men of his ferocious and generous age. He, who massacred the garrison at San José in cold blood, was centuries ahead of his time in his treatment of the natives of Guiana. He alleged that this was only to win them from the Spaniard, and to make the conquest of Guiana an easy matter. But the standard of behaviour which he adopted for this very prudent purpose was not that which would have occurred to a lesser man. He paid liberally all those pressed into his service as guides, and he would not permit his men to touch any goods without payment. Still less would he allow them to touch the women: whereas the Spaniards had made free with both. The impression was such that the Indians welcomed him after more than twenty years' interval and offered to make him their king. Yet he professed no higher motive than self-interest.

He did of course make it clear that power, and not wealth, was what he sought. The voyage was undertaken for the glory of Elizabeth and the enlarging of her empire. It was objected against him that he had not bestirred himself to spoil the Spaniard. He replied:

It became not the former fortune in which I once lived, to go journeys of Picory: it had sorted ill with the offices of Honour, which by her Majesty's grace, I hold this day in England, to run from cape to cape and from place to place, for the pillage of ordinarie prizes....[8]

Nevertheless, having sufficient opportunity to take Don Antonio de Berreo, who the year before had ambushed seven men of his, he felt "I should have savoured very much of the Ass" not to capture him and set the town of San José on fire. Don Antonio, turning out to be a very sufficient gentleman, was afterwards of great assistance to Ralegh in exploring the Orinoco.

However, it was customary to respect birth in an enemy. Ralegh would treat anyone with the same mixture of generosity and ruthlessness. Religious persecution horrified him: in the Preface to the *History of the World*, he remarks that "there is nothing more to be admired and more to be lamented than the private contention, the passionate disputes, the personal hatred and the perpetual war, massacre and murders for religion among Christians". He was prepared to take risks and to overcome personal interests in the cause of liberty of conscience. In 1593 he made a notable speech in defence of the Brownists in the House of Commons. In 1594 he sat up all night talking with the Jesuit John Cornelius who was imprisoned for his faith, whereas in 1591 he had championed the imprisoned Puritan John Udall, and even joined forces with Essex to petition the queen for him.

As Ralegh's appetite for knowledge led him to an interest and tolerance for many different beliefs, it sharpened his contempt for dogmatism in all its forms. He delighted to expose the smug cleric, or bait the plain man. Those who took refuge in authority would not escape; "for myself, I shall never be persuaded that God hath shut up all light of learning within the lanthorn of Aristotle's brains",[9] he remarked. In his jesting mood he would occasionally forget diplomacy and say outrageous things: King James might have forgiven him the introduction of smoking had not Ralegh snubbed him at their first meeting. There was a wordy and unenlightened divine in attendance on Ralegh at his execution, whom he befooled and be-mused with mock sententiousness and scandalized with a pipe of tobacco. And though he wrote one epitaph for himself majestic in its pomp and resigna-tion, he also tossed off a squib on the snuff of a candle:

> Cowards fear to die: but courage stout,
> Rather than live in snuff, will be put out.

His work reflected every side of his personality faithfully and there are literary parallels to that streak of brutality and calculation which came out in his campaigning. This is quite different from his habit of mixing up worldly and spiritual instructions, as in the famous last letter to his wife, a habit he shared with Thomas More and many other less remarkable men of the sixteenth century. They were not too fine to think it a matter unworthy of their last hours to provide for their family. Ralegh was never gross: but he was, like Marlowe, "of a cruel heart". He was responsible for carrying out one of the most brutal acts of war in his time, the Massacre of Smerwick: and his pleasant little poem to his son, *Three things there be*, would hardly be approved of by modern psychology:

...And they be these, the wood, the weed, the wagg,
The wood is that which makes the gallows tree,
The weed is that which strings the Hangman's bag,
The wagg my pritty knave betokeneth thee....

When James brought Ralegh himself to the block in 1618 the same vein prompted his last piece of *panache*, the cry to the headsman: "What dost fear? Strike, man, strike!"

Ralegh's cruelty was the reverse side of his courage and both have glamour enough. But his statist's vein can be disconcerting to the hero-worshipper. More than one writer on Ralegh has been troubled by the tone of some of his writings, such as *The Maxims of State* and *The Advice to His Son*. Their trite worldly wisdom seems incompatible with the tone of his better work. But that better work depends precisely upon an unconscious flexibility and a capacity to live and think upon many different levels. His worse writings are the price to be paid for it: they show the defects of his qualities. Ralegh's worldly interests were met in a worldly spirit, just as Shakespeare drove hard bargains and did not readily forgive his debtors.

47

"What shocks the moral philosopher delights the chameleon poet"; it was no impoverishment of their poetry.

Of course Ralegh's powers were too well adjusted for him to be conscious of their effects. If he sat between wind and tide, it was largely by an instinctive power of self-adaptation. Like the movement of a great athlete or a fine dancer, it was a matter of skill and not of calculation. He was no schemer after the school of Francis Bacon. His writing depends upon unconsciousness of flexibility, and thereby gains half its grace. Take for example this section from *The Discovery of Guiana*:[10]

On both sides of the river we passed the most beautiful country that ever mine eyes beheld...the grasse short and green, and in divers parts groves of trees by themselves, as if they had been by all the art and labour in the world so made of purpose: and still as we rowed, the deere came down feeding by the water side, as if they had been used to a keeper's call.

The power of the passage depends on its sudden flow of gentleness: and this depends on Ralegh not recognizing the reason why the deer coming down so take his eye and his heart. The tameness of the deer in that strange country, and the ordered beauty of the landscape, produced a wave of home-sickness: the wave rose and fell but it did not break: and Ralegh passes on to "great store of fowles of many sortes" and "divers sortes of strange fish and of marvellous bigness" with no sense of a drop.

Ralegh's instinct for keeping his writing transparent in this way is probably the chief cause of its strength. The letter which he wrote to his wife before the mock execution at Winchester in 1603 is deservedly famous, but it has not the unstudied power of the one he wrote from the Indies, after his son had been killed on the last voyage. The letter is short, but afterwards Ralegh added a postscript of three or four times the length in which he poured out the story. The letter runs:[11]

I was loathe to write because I knew not how to comfort you; and God knows I never knew what sorrow meant till now. All that I can say to you is this: that you must obey the will and providence of God; and remember that the Queen's Majesty bare the loss of Prince Henry with a magnanimous spirit, as the lady Harrington of her only son. Comfort your heart (dear Bess), I shall sorrow for us both: and I shall sorrow the less because I have not long to sorrow, because not long to live. I refer you to Mr Secretary Winwood's letter, who will give you a copy of it if you send for it: therein you shall know what hath passed. I have written but that letter, for my brains are broken and it is a torment to me to write, and especially of misery.... I have cleansed my ship of sick men and sent them home; and hope that God will send us somewhat before we return.

And the postscript:

I protest before the majesty of God that as Sir Francis Drake and Sir John Hawkins died heartbroken when they failed of their enterprise, I could willingly do the like, did I not contend with sorrow to comfort and relieve you.... My brains are broken and I cannot write much: I live yet and I have told you why.... I am sure there is never a base slave in all the fleet hath taken the pains and care that I have done, that hath slept so little and travailed so much: my friends will not believe them; and for the rest I care not; God in heaven bless you and strengthen your heart.

# III

# THE SCHOOL OF NIGHT

## THE DOCTRINE

We have not strength to open our mental eyes, and to behold the beauty of the Good, that incorruptible beauty which no tongue can tell. Then only will you see it, when you cannot speak of it: for the knowledge of it is deep silence and the suppression of all the senses.

TRISMEGISTUS, *The Key*.

The doctrine of the School of Night was, and has remained, a matter in which all outsiders are Peeping Toms. The evidence is of very differing levels of plausibility: for instance, few of Ralegh's writings can be dated, and had we not proof of the fixity of his opinions in other directions, it would be mere folly to quote them as any likely indication of the kind of thing his club discussed.

The esotericism of the school was partly due to necessity. The public attitude towards free intellectual enquiry has been already mentioned: there was actual danger in too aspiring a mind. Secondly, much of Harriot's astronomy must have appeared incomprehensible to the generality, with a result quite opposite to that which the modern astronomer may look for. Thirdly, there does seem to have been a strong tinge of the occult in the school. Fourthly, some of the members were of a haughty and self-sufficient spirit, and not averse from accepting the popular verdict that they were not as other men.

Such evidence as there is may be divided into two kinds: the writings of the school, and their reported speeches, their general reputation and the parodies of their doctrine which the rival group put forth. When the first kind of evidence is corroborated by the second, the case is at its strongest: either kind alone is about of equal weight, for the chances of distortion in report or caricature fully balance the chronological uncertainties of the writings of the school.

Ralegh has left some half a dozen short prose treatises which show his views on religion, science and politics. Marlowe has left his plays where (particularly in *Tamburlaine* and *Dr Faustus*) the doctrinal element is strong and easily isolated, but as dramatic poetry, the evidence is not so direct as Ralegh's. Chapman has left a body of purely doctrinal poetry, as well as his plays, but its complexity and his semi-isolation make it of no stronger value than Marlowe's. Harriot is the one whose views would probably have united and correlated all the others: it is therefore all the harder that no relevant work of his survives.

To begin with Ralegh, and with his religious writing: there is *The Soul*, which throws an added charm over the recollection of the conversation with the Rev. Ralph Ironside. It is a sufficient proof that Ralegh was no atheist in the modern sense, nor, as Aubrey asserted, "a-Christ", i.e. a Socinian. His discourse is set out under seven heads: it begins with a borrowing from the "obscure and intricate" Aristotle (*De Anima*, 2. 20–30). The treatise is thick-sown with quotations from the Scriptures and the Fathers: indeed the method of argument is chiefly by citation of texts.

# THE DOCTRINE

Ralegh divides the soul into three parts: the vege-
table, animal and reasonable (compare Donne's "My
second soul of sense and first of growth"). The souls of
beasts are "as it were drowned in the blood" and reach
only to consciousness of "things present earthly and
such as are before their eyes" (compare *Dr Faustus*,
5. 2. 177–83: "Why wast thou not a creature wanting soul?"). The substance of the soul is not identical
with the Divine Nature for it can exist apart from
virtue:

Our souls are just and wise and patient: yet because
they may be without these things, therefore they are
not these things, and are compounded: simple indeed
they may be in respect of the elements and of the bodies
that are made of them: but in respect of God they are
compounded: and therefore cannot be of the substance
of God.[1]

Christ was of the substance of God: man is made
"not in substance the same, but like in quality". As
it gives life to the body, this semi-divine substance is
called a soul: as it will continue to live and be apart
from the body, it is spirit.

Ralegh rejects Origen's theory of the simultaneous
creation of all souls, for when created they must be
active: "souls cannot sleep like dormice". The functions of the soul are then described: they consist of the
instincts, the senses, the emotions, and the functions

55

of the Reasonable Soul, which are Understanding and Will.

The habitation of the soul is discussed at length according to Plato, Aristotle, Augustine, and others: but Ralegh decides for himself that it is in the whole body "not as a mariner in a ship, but being present everywhere".[2]

Finally he argues for the immortality of the soul from its innate religious sense: a splendid *non-sequitur*: "all wise men have ever minded godliness and virtue with the study of wisdom". And having soared to this height, he ends regrettably but characteristically with the plea that there must be a future life to redress the balance of this one, and give the deserving what they have earned.

The treatise on *The Soul* is of no great originality, nor, except for a few passages, is it lit up with the blaze which Ralegh could kindle upon the great commonplaces. It shows that Ralegh had thought conscientiously on recognized lines: that he weighed orthodoxy before he found it wanting, and that he was familiar with the Scriptures and the Fathers as instruments of enquiry. The treatise reveals his interests rather than his accomplishments, and it demonstrates negatively that doctrinal theology was not his strong point.

A surer proof of his religious sense is in the words to his wife before the mock execution of 1603, or the epitaph which he adapted from an early song of his own and in which, as Chambers puts it, "the rumoured atheist, at the close of his long voyage, casts anchor beside the Jesuit Southwell":[3]

> Even such is Time, which takes in trust
> Our Youth, our Joys and all we have,
> And pays us but with age and dust,
> Who in the dark and silent grave
> When we have wandered all our wayes
> Shutts up the story of our days:
> And from which Earth, and Grave, and Dust,
> The Lord shall raise me up I trust.

It has been said that any Elizabethan could write greatly when he wrote on death: it might also be said that no Elizabethan could write impersonally on death, that their comparatively exaggerated sense of individuality gave them an exaggerated sense of the horrors of dissolution which a less egoistic age might not feel. In any case it is difficult to discover much interplay between Ralegh's passionate religious sense and his meddling intellect. It would be an undue simplification to say that, unable to bear the negative results of his intellectual voyaging, he fell back upon a purely emotional assertion. It was rather that the intellect, as it was exercised in philosophy and the sciences at that time, was an instrument of rationalization rather than of reason: and that Ralegh, like other men of his age, was capable of accepting more than he could erect into a schema.

A man with Ralegh's extraordinary sensibility to mood and powers of sympathetic projection was ill qualified to learn philosophy *via* "the mathematics": and though he eventually assimilated his work, "turning all into honey, working all into one relish and savour", the first effect was to make him unnaturally stiff and stilted.

*The Sceptic* is a good deal more interesting. Here Ralegh was concerned with epistemology and not religion. In this work Ralegh showed himself abreast of his time; he is foreshadowing Bacon. The treatise is mainly concerned with the relation of sense-data to the external world. Ralegh begins by pointing out that the widely differing structure of the animals makes it probable that their sense-data vary. This applies to all the five senses. Also our own sense-data vary with regard to the same object according to conditions, e.g. distorting spectacles alter our vision.

We have no reason to believe that our sense-data are in any way a better representation of the object "in its own nature" than those of the animals.

Ralegh then digresses upon the fact that animals can communicate with each other, and also appear to have elementary reasoning powers, so that human standards are not absolute in these spheres either.

## THE DOCTRINE

The mental reactions of men differ as much as their sense perceptions: *quot homines, tot sententiae*. We have no means of arbitrating finally between Plato and Epicurus.

Ralegh returns to sense-perception. The different senses may be only different channels through which one attribute of the object presents itself diversely. Or, conversely, they may represent different attributes, and there may be others which we do not perceive because we have not the sensuous equipment to do so.[4]

Finally, if it is objected that Nature has ordered these things, and must have arranged that our senses and the external world shall be exactly adapted to each other, Ralegh will ask, What Nature? for there is a controversy about the nature of Nature, philosophers disagree, and he has no means of establishing what Nature is.

It will be realized that Ralegh has practically reduced himself to solipsism. The argument is probably Harriot's, and it has all the merits and defects of a piece of pioneer work. Bacon had not yet begun to write, and however elementary the points raised by Ralegh, his method is admirable. He starts from observation; the different methods of generation among beasts are cited at great length: he notes that a dog, following the chase to a way where three paths fork, will smell the first and second path, and, if he draws blank, will take the third without examination, which argues a kind of reasoning. He experiments upon himself, trying the effect of stopping both his ears, or only one ear, etc.; and all with the same enthusiasm as he explored America, missing nothing from the oysters to the pineapples.

*The Sceptic* also shows Ralegh's powers of sympathetic projection. This was an age when animals were brutally treated, and perhaps Ralegh enjoyed bear-baiting himself, yet he could write:

Why should I presume to prefer my conceit and imagination in affirming that a thing is thus and thus in its own nature, before the conceit of other living creatures who may as well think it to be otherwise in their own natures, because it appeareth otherwise to them than it doth to me?

They are living creatures as well as I: why should I condemn their conceit and phantasy concerning anything, more than they may mine?

Perhaps it was only in a purely speculative way that Ralegh was prepared to dethrone man from the lordship of creation: there were few who would have gone with him as far as that. Certainly it is not unconnected with his practical way of showing that the American Indians were part of the human race, which the Spaniards seem hardly to have conceded (or indeed his own countrymen).

# THE DOCTRINE

The preface to the *History of the World* reiterates the substance of *The Sceptic* in a condensed form. "Nature triumpheth in dissimilitude" both of "visible forms and shapes" and of "forms internall". And as Nature shows a continual variety of forms, so Fortune delights to toss men from one extreme to the other.

Change of fortune in the great theatre is but as change of garments in the less, for when on the one and the other, every man wears but his own skin, the players are all alike.[5]

This reads almost like a paraphrase of the Mutabilitie Cantos.

Ralegh goes on to belittle human knowledge: the workings of cause and effect are known to all; "the cheesewife knoweth as well as the philosopher that sour runnet doth coagulate her milk into a curd", but neither the one nor the other can go beyond this, and explain why it should be so. Man, "that no sooner begins to learn than to die, that hath in his memory but borrowed knowledge, in his understanding nothing truly, that is ignorant of the essence of his own soul", must acknowledge himself to be "an idiot in the next cause of his own life" and lay aside all hope of intellectual certainty.[6]

But the testimony of the learned Heathen, as well as of the Church, points beyond the intellect to "an eternal and infinite being". Ralegh gathers them up in a magnificent simile:

Certainly, as all the rivers in the world, though they have divers risings and divers runnings, though they sometimes hide themselves for awhile under ground and seem to be lost in the sea-like lakes, do at last find and fall into the great ocean: so after all the searches that human capacity hath and after all philosophical contemplation and curiosity, in the necessity of this infinite power all the reason of man ends and dissolves itself.

The labyrinthine sentence unfolds and flows, rising to its climax just before the end, and ebbing away in a hush: it has the movement of the river it describes. Ralegh is drawing on his own experience of 500 miles of the Orinoco.

How different in tone and accent from Bacon's

We must quit the small vessel of human reason and put ourselves on board the ship of the Church, which alone possesses the divine needle for justly shaping the course.

To abandon reason in so reasonable and methodical a fashion savours more than a little of "that brisk lad, Ignorance", and it is not very surprising to find Bacon, however unconscious of irony, concluding:

And therefore the more absurd and incredible any divine mystery is, the greater honour we do to God in believing it: and so much the more noble the victory of faith.[7]

Hobbes is just around the corner. "Bacon's desire to separate religious truth and scientific truth was in the interests of science, not of religion. He wished to *keep science pure from religion.*"[8] Ralegh and his circle had no bias: they could afford to be more sceptical of the letter of Christianity for that very reason. They did not "quit" reason: it became subsumed under something more comprehensive, the wisdom of the full man.

Non aspettar mio dir più, ni mio cenno,
Libro, dritto e sano è tuo arbitrio,
E falla fora non fare a suo senno:
Per ch'io te sopra te corono e mitro.

There was no danger of not rendering unto Caesar the things that are Caesar's: for Ralegh shared the view of More and Erasmus that God had disclosed Himself in the creation of the world, as well as in revelation by grace, and that, therefore, the study of second causes was a religious duty. But there was no temptation to confuse the first cause and the second.

At his death Ralegh "spoke much of the great and incomprehensible God", and he opens the first chapters of the *History of the World* with a credo:

God, whom the wisest men acknowledge to be a power ineffable and virtue infinite: a light by abundant clarity invisible: an understanding which only itself can comprehend: an essence eternal and spiritual, of absolute pureness and simplicity: was and is pleased to make Himself known by the work of the world....

But Ralegh had admitted that the creation was not to be understood. Nor did he fret himself over the limitations of human reason, or deny the value of what knowledge man might be able to get for himself. He possessed the faculty which Keats thought of the first necessity for a man of achievement, "negative capability, that is, when a man is capable of being in uncertainties, mysteries, doubts, without any irritable reaching after fact and reason".[9] And he was in no danger of confusing different universes of discourse. He recognized that most knowledge had only a limited sphere of application:

The quantity we have is of the body: we are by it joined to the earth: we are compounded of the earth: and we inhabit it. The heavens are high, far off and unsearchable: we have sense and feeling of corporal things, and of eternal grace but by revelation.[10]

The consequence of this separation of different levels of knowledge had a practical corollary. Ralegh was tolerant in a fanatical age, for he held that all opinions were only schema. It was also quite easy for him to hold two incompatible views without any irritation, and to mix his motives in a way which may seem reprehensible in a more consistent age. It can be related to his poetry as well, to the way in which the symbol of Cynthia unites so many different figures, and co-ordinates so many different facets of experience. The combination of an insatiate thirst for knowledge with a flexibility which allows the mind to adopt many different points of view is not a common thing: but Marlowe shared it with Ralegh. He could write *Dr Faustus* and *Hero and Leander* within a year or two of each other, perhaps within the same year.

Scepticism left the school with no alternative to a Transcendental God: "the God that sits in Heaven" as Marlowe put it. Even William Warner, who gave up the thirteenth book of *Albion's England* to "Physics and Ethics against Atheists and Epicures", spent all his time putting the case for a God above Nature, and shuffled off the Trinity with a promise to write of it some other time. In a passage which recalls Ralegh's simile of the ocean he wrote:

To one Sea-flow all Fluds, one Sunne enlighteneth
   every light,
Of all celestial Movings is One-Mover, Artists
   write.
Trunk, bark, boughs, leaves and blossoms, none like
   other, hath a tree;
Yet but one Root, whence all: which but one author's
   Act can be.[11]

God is to be defined by negatives and to be separated from Nature and from human knowledge.[12]

Unmovable, unchangeable, 'bove nature, unbegot,
Unpassive, unmateriall, uncompounded, Infinite
In Spirit, not in Body, nor in Quantity but Might....
Lord, Darkness is thy Covert, in thine outer Courts
    I tire....

The consequence of this was to make the world of phenomena a small and alien thing: Nature was subject to Time and Change, ruled by Mutabilitie. Philosophy was not to be approached through Nature: for nothing was clearly established in the world of the senses. Nevertheless, science, since it gave a measure of control over Nature, was to be cultivated, and if possible correlated with philosophy. The link was in the oldest and most developed of the sciences, that of astronomy: for here religion was involved.

When I behold the heavens, then I repent,

said Faustus. He questions Mephistopheles of Hell and where it is to be found: and Mephistopheles, reconciling Copernicus and Christianity in Marlowe's mightiest line, answered:

Why, this is Hell, nor am I out of it.

In the sixteenth century, astronomical discovery was as disturbing as Darwinianism in the nineteenth: and with much of the same disproportionate effect

66

upon religious thought. It seemed to many as though Christianity were bound up with the medieval cosmogony.

The necessity for a Transcendental God was due to the sudden enlargement of the universe, as the telescope of Harriot revealed it, in the sense in which Hardy's doctrine of the Immanent Will was forced upon him by the pseudo-scientific attitude of *Two On a Tower* and *The Dynasts*. The School of Night therefore sought "a Philosophic Theology" and for this purpose they turned to the classics for help in the synthesis. They were driven to those early writers whose sayings were most conveniently to be adapted to their own situation. They began with Stoicism, the fashionable and almost inevitable philosophy of the time: the stoicism of Plutarch and Seneca. But the Stoics had included a good deal of the doctrine of such esoteric writers as Heraclitus of Ephesus and his sayings can be divined behind the poetry of Marlowe, Chapman and Ralegh. Heraclitus' doctrine of the Eternal Fire was particularly congenial to astronomers.

It has been urged that the Stoicism of the sixteenth century was not a philosophy but a kind of insurance policy against disaster.[13] It is certain that the School of Night would not interpret their teachers with notable detachment. In spite of protestations that philosophy was the Divine Skill, they seem to have used it as raw

67

·material for poetry; which resulted in some rather unphilosophical philosophy and some very great poetry.

The influence of Heraclitus and the Stoics is most plainly seen in their cosmogony and their theory of the soul. Both held that fire, heat and motion were ultimately identical and were the source of all life. Fire is divine and the first of all elements:[14] the other elements all contain some proportion of fire. Air is the next highest of the elements, and the spirit of man is made of air and fire,[15] but fire is its substance.[16]

Air and fire tend upwards: hence the upright carriage of man's body indicates his divine nature.[17] Nevertheless, though the body may be subdued to the soul, it may also corrupt the soul; and the senses, in particular the eye, will lead man astray if they are not disciplined.[18]

The senses record only the continual flux of the external world,[19] yet "such change is for Heraclitus the reality which forms the very structure of things. It is not change, but changing, and the changing is Fire. For fire never rests and it is the element of animation which engenders all and consumes all".[20]

Heraclitus' theory of the "durable fire" veiled and hid by the temporal flux was taken over by Marlowe and Chapman and Ralegh, not as a philosophic conception but as a poetic symbol. They did not strictly co-ordinate these symbols with their own philosophy but used them simultaneously. All three were very ready to take their own "raptures" as inspired. They were certainly at one with Heraclitus in their disdain of the mob.[21] Marlowe scorned "rhyming mother wits" and any other kind of "base fellow". Chapman despised the blindness of most men, and Ralegh was "damnable proud". Yet they were equally remarkable for their freedom from any social snobbery. Marlowe insisted again and again that "virtue is the true nobility", Chapman had very heterodox views on the relations of kings and subjects, and little respect for blood: and Ralegh compared the Indian women of Guiana to the ladies of the Court and found them almost indistinguishable.

This haughtiness and sense of separation from the multitude was a mark of Renaissance Stoicism. In England it is at its worst in the plays of Marston: but it is to be found in Ben Jonson and even in Michael Drayton. The poets probably felt it as a consequence of their office. They were accorded sacred revelations, not given to common men. The doctrines of inspiration and of Furor Poeticus were very widespread.

Stoicism was no doubt more of a religion than a philosophy even in classical times. It was very weak on the side of metaphysics: its contribution to the main stream of philosophic development was ethical.

## THE SCHOOL OF NIGHT

The School of Night stressed its metaphysics, its most poetic and least philosophic aspect: consequently they were not so obviously "metaphysical" as other writers.

In addition to philosophic speculation, the school must have dabbled in the occult. Magic symbols appear too frequently to be the result of coincidence. Chapman seems familiar with the practice and doctrines of necromancy, although he is the most devout of the group. The combination may seem very unnatural and improbable, but the spread of interest in the occult was in fact closely allied to philosophy and science. Pico della Mirandola had been interested in the Hermetic writings and the Cabbala. Hermeticism prompted Cornelius Agrippa's *De Occulta Philosophica*, in which he tried to reconcile Hermes and orthodox Christianity. "The studies also of natural science and of medicine were implicated with the Hermetic theories, dangerous and unsuitable as these had been considered by the orthodox in religion and science. Many minor Hermetists made allegory of their alchemy, explaining their 'mystery' in terms of the Christian mystery."[22]

It may also be relevant to recall the peculiar tangle of orthodox Christianity and the occult which Professor Saurat has revealed in the writings of Milton.

The difficulty of sifting the astronomer from the astrologer, and philosophy from necromancy was the task of the seventeenth century rather than the sixteenth. If a horoscope were really to be trusted, to cast it was just as respectable as to read Plato. The mass of erudition which had been let loose on Europe by the liberating forces of the previous century was quite unorganized and very miscellaneous; the best of scholars were still at sea.

A good many symbols of the occult writers are also ✓ those of the Church. For instance, the Two Eyes of the Soul, with which Hermes is so much concerned, are found in Origen (*Contra Celsum*, VII, 39), in the *Theologica Germanica* (chapter VII) and in Meister Eckhardt (ed. Pfeiffer, 110, 21–5).[23] The Sun God and the Moon Goddess are an alternative way of expressing the same opposition between the Active and the Contemplative life, living in Time and living in Eternity.[24] They are used by Marlowe and Chapman: also some of the commoner Beast Symbols. Ralegh cites Hermes, who was translated by Ficino, and therefore probably known to Chapman also. There are also passages in Dionysius the Areopagite which recall *The Shadow of Night*.[25]

Although the poets were of diverse tastes they all seem to have been interested in Harriot's astronomy. It was but a little step from astronomy to astrology and though Harriot seems to have quite shared the modern scientist's attitude in these matters, he could not control the associations which his subject might have in the minds of the poets. In Marlowe it linked itself with epistemology: in Chapman with the occult. Harriot, after all, though in some sense the master of the school, was not actually in charge of it. The discussions may not always have followed his lines, or been confined to the subjects in which he was interested.

It is, for instance, probable that a certain amount of politics and statecraft entered in. They were naturally absorbing topics to Ralegh. Northumberland was an Italian scholar, and Marlowe had evidently read Machiavelli, at least. Ralegh adopted his "policy", for it has recently been shown that *The Maxims of State* and *Cabinet Counsel* are little more than compilations from Machiavelli's *Il Principe* and *Discorsi*, Guicciardini and Jean Bodin.[26]

Machiavelli was equated with the devil and to have studied him at all was almost as heinous as to have glanced at the Scriptures. The plain man was bewildered by the gap between diplomatic and private standards of behaviour, which Machiavelli implied. Though his own behaviour might in fact be based upon such assumptions, it was intolerable to have such things openly set forth. Marlowe made satiric play upon this in his treatment of the Christians in *The Jew of Malta*, where Machiavelli as Prologue says,

# THE DOCTRINE

Admired I am of those that hate me most.
Though some speak openly against my books,
Yet will they read me....

This happens to be an exact description of Ralegh.
It must have given him great pleasure, when he had
quoted Machiavelli quite literally for several para-
graphs, to remark, "Whereby appeareth the false
doctrine of the Machiavellian policy". Throughout
*The Maxims of State* he borrows from Machiavelli and
denounces his writings in a regular sequence: the more
exact the citation, the more stern his denunciations.

These maxims came fairly late in Ralegh's career:
but he had been attacked as a Machiavel from his
earliest rise to favour. It was particularly fitting that
he should demonstrate the thoroughness of his training
in his treatment of the teacher.

Both Marlowe and Chapman had been influenced
by Machiavelli in a similar way. Of course he was a
fashion among intellectuals, rather as Marx is to-day.
Both of the poets attacked "Machiavellianism" (i.e.
the popular perversion of his doctrine which passed
current in England), not in a spirit of outraged
morality, as most of their contemporaries did: on the
contrary in a very Machiavellian way; by borrowing
as much of his doctrine as they needed and holding
the rest up to ridicule. Instead of anathema, they
used satire. This is not the place to go into the propor-

73

tion of "Machiavellianism" and anti-Machiavellianism in *The Jew of Malta* and *All Fools*. Barabas puts the case for "Machiavellianism":

> Haply some hapless man hath conscience,
> And for his conscience lives in beggary...,

whilst at the same time the proportions in which he is drawn are an implicit "placing" of the doctrine. Again and again, Chapman reduces the Machiavels—Baligny, La Fin, Ravel, Gostanzo—to something petty and ineffectual even in success. The essential unintelligence and short-sightedness of sharp practice, the self-blinding of the man who professes to know the world, are among the central themes of all Chapman's work and cannot be dealt with at the end of a chapter. The relationship of his work to Machiavelli and to "Machiavellianism" is a subject which would require and repay a separate study.

# IV

## SIR WALTER RALEGH

### *COURTIER AND COURT POET*

His song was all a lamentable lay
Of great unkindness and of usage hard
Of Cynthia, the Ladie of the Sea,
Which from her presence faultless him debarred.
And ever and anon with singults rife
He cryed out, to make his undersong:
"Ah, my love's queen and goddess of my life,
Who shall me pity, when thou dost me wrong?"

EDMUND SPENSER, *Colin Clout's Come Home Again.*

From the fragments of Ralegh's verse which survive, it is plain that he developed as a poet between 1580 and 1590, and still more rapidly in the next decade. But in 1580 he was already nearing thirty years of age, and had been writing for some time. The interest of his verse is largely in the way in which it keeps some of the habits of the earlier writers like Wyatt (who had been buried at Sherborne ten years before Ralegh was born), and yet foreshadows later developments. It is new wine poured into old bottles.

In this respect he resembles his friend Sidney: but Sidney died too soon for the cross-currents to become eddies in his verse. Fulke Greville too was of their generation: but his writing was not in the main stream at all.

Ralegh's earliest poems were exercises in the use of "figures", and patterns. Puttenham quoted him to illustrate "the Underlay or Cuckoe Spell" and "Ploche or the Doubler", taking for this the last lines of *The Excuse*:

> Yet when I saw myself to you was true,
> I loved myself, because myself loved you.

This poetry had hardly reached the decorative stage of pastoral imagery which belongs to the mid-1580's, when the attitude defined by Coleridge began to prevail:

The imagery is almost always general: sun, moon, flowers, breezes, murmuring streams, warbling songsters... the fable of their narrative poems, for the most part drawn from mythology, or sources of equal notoriety, derive their chief attractions from the manner of treating them: from impassioned flow or picturesque arrangement.... The excellence at which they aimed, consisted in the exquisite polish of the diction, combined with perfect simplicity... by the studied position of words and phrases, so that *not only each part should be melodious in itself, but contribute to the harmony of the whole*, each note referring and conducing to the melody of all the foregoing and following words of the same period or stanza: and lastly, with equal labour, the greater because unbetrayed, by *the variation and various harmonies of their metrical movement*... by countless modifications and subtle balances of sound in the common metres of their country.[1]

If the passages I have stressed are reflectively considered it will be obvious how discriminating is Coleridge's judgment, and what a great achievement the early Elizabethan style really was. These writers carried out a work quite as heavy, though less noticeable, than that of their successors: and the new lyric school of the nineties was only possible because foundations had been laid for it. In bringing rhythmic forms to a greater flexibility and resilience, and in developing a pure and sonorous vocabulary, they prepared the way for the rich complexity of the dramatists and the "metaphysicals". The revolt from what later seemed a heavy and formal way of writing was partly the result of the greater malleability and stability of the language which that style had brought about, and which offered a firm basis for variation and experiment.

Ralegh was one of the pioneers. His characteristic accent, representing his technical contribution to English verse, was slow and emphatic, open vowels weighted by rich alliteration:

> Oblivion laid him down on Laura's hearse.

But he did not always move in such heavy brocade: in his songs he developed varieties of tempo rather than sound-patterns. *The Lie*, for instance, is built on parallel clauses and a slightly varied refrain, which comes in at the end of each stanza like a dagger thrust, and emphasizes the brute energy of the vituperation. The matter of the poems shifts more in the method of approach than in the method of presentation. By control of the tempo (i.e. "total rhythm"), Ralegh gets all the contrasts which a later poet would have expressed by imagery or description:

> Say to the Court it glows
> And shines like rotten wood,
> Say to the Church it shows
> What's good and does no good.
> If Church and Court reply,
> Then give them both the lie....

Tell zeal it wants devotion,
Tell love it is but lust,
Tell time it meets but motion,
Tell flesh it is but dust.
And wish them not reply,
For thou must give the lie....

So when thou hast, as I
Commanded thee, done blabbing,
Because to give the lie
Deserves no less than stabbing,
Stab at thee he that will,
No stab thy soul can kill.

It was no mean achievement to keep up for thirteen stanzas this unprogressive fury, like a racing motor-boat cutting circles round a buoy. Apart from the personal qualities necessary, it requires a comparatively tough and inflexible texture in the language. The merit of the poem lies in the way in which slight variations are introduced, which enrich and widen its scope without detracting from the cumulative effect. It is an interesting exercise to compare this with Nashe's *Adieu, farewell earth's bliss*,[2] where the technique is very similar, but the work is more uneven: some of the aspects predominate. Nashe's poem is not remembered as a whole, but chiefly for the stanza

Brightness falls from the air,
Queens have died young, and fair:
Dust hath closed Helen's eye.

Both poems may be contrasted with Marvell's *To His Coy Mistress*, where the variations are much more strongly marked.

In the three stanzas quoted from Ralegh, the first is a frontal attack: the monosyllables and the imagery are crisp with contempt. The second is softened: the lines are lingered out by "devotion" and "motion", the refrain has not its usual force. The third stanza begins with the irony suddenly inverted and turned upon himself, and his "blabbing", unpacking his heart in words: it ends in magnificent self-assertion. Ralegh has forgotten his enmities to exult in the sense of power his diatribe has produced.

The poem is in the manner of his best middle work. He used similar methods in his praise of Elizabeth, as for instance in *Praisd be Diana's Fair and Harmless Light*. This begins with a kind of choric chant, which has no variations, but beats out the metre: it rises to the complexity of

> Time wears her not, she doth his chariot guide,
> Mortalitie below her orb is plaste,
> By her the virtues of the stars down slide,
> In her is virtue's perfect image cast.

The first line has a beautiful image of the outstripping in the balance of the slow opening clause against its quicker-moving successor, and the movement is steadied up by the stately second line. Then the ambiguity of "virtue" works up a balance of another kind: the first, physical "virtue" is radiant, the second, moral "virtue" is fixed like a stone. These lines foreshadow his greater poem, where Mortality and the Stars are to be his theme.

Ralegh had always affected the rôle of the silent lover, whose respect and awe kept his passion under, to gnaw viperously in his breast: "Fain would I, but I dare not" was his note. His imprisonment allowed him to gain the full benefits of contrast, and to draw on the effect of his past reserve. Now, of course, he could no longer restrain his feelings. When Elizabeth was rowed down the Thames past the Tower, he asked his keeper (who happened to be his Cornish kinsman, George Carew) that he might be disguised as a poor waterman and rowed near enough to catch a glimpse of her. When Carew refused he became dangerously lunatic, and fell upon him with a knife. Sir Arthur Gorges, who was paying the prisoner a visit, had to intervene when he saw "the iron walking" in this way, and received a slash across the knuckles before Ralegh was overpowered. Of course he could not be expected to hold his tongue about such a violent affair, and he wrote a harrowing description of it to Cecil, adding "Sir W. R. will shortly grow to be Orlando Furioso if the bright Angelica persevere against him a little longer".

# COURTIER AND COURT POET

Poetry was poured out in an effort to move implacable majesty: and for the most part it has a new note. Ralegh does not give up any of his symbols and images, but his tone changes under the pressure of adversity. His best verse belongs to these years of disgrace; and unlike the professional poet Ralegh did not need, or insist, that he should go on writing poetry when he was no longer capable of his best.

It was necessary to reverse the pastoralism and Ralegh took up the rôle of the Hermit, the recognized one for a blighted lover. (Compare the hermitess Clorin in Fletcher's *Faithful Shepherdess*.) There is his own poem, *Like to a Hermit poor in place obscure*, where he describes his food of sorrow, his drink of tears, his staff of broken hope, and his couch of "late repentance linked with long desire". There is Spenser's long and elaborate account of how Timias became a hermit and lived almost as a madman (*The Faerie Queene*, IV, VII, XXXVIII–XLVII). He chose a "gloomy glade" full of "sad melancholy". He rent his clothes and let his hair grow "uncomb'd, uncurled, and carelessly unshed". *Walsingham* is also suggestive of palmers and hermits and it has another and more direct connection with this period.

The rôle of hermit was an ingenious one. It was a tactful way of reminding Elizabeth of his imprisonment and banishment: it completely obliterated the awkward fact of the existence of Lady Ralegh.

The Hermit was to live in an "obscured shade",

> a gloomy glade
> Where hardly eye mote see bright heaven's face
> For mossy trees which covered all with shade
> And sad melancholy: there he his cabin made,

or as Chapman put it, where there were

> Virtues obscured and banished the day
> With all the glories of this spongie sway:
> Prisoned in flesh, and that poor flesh in bands
> Of stone and steel, chief flowers of virtue's garlands....
> Ye living spirits then, if any live
> Whom like extremes do like afflictions give,
> Shun, shun this cruel light, and end your thrall
> In these soft shades of sable funeral....

The pastoral conceit, with a little ingenuity, could sometimes be made to fit the occasion directly. Ralegh was drawing on his court poetry when he wrote to Cecil, on the queen's departure on progress:

My heart was never broken till this day, that I hear the Queen goes away so far off, whom I have followed so many years with so great love and desire, in so many journeys, and am now left behind her in a dark prison all alone.... I that was wont to behold her riding like Alexander, hunting like Diana, walking like Venus, the gentle wind blowing her fair hair about her pure cheeks like a nymph, sometimes sitting in the shade like a Goddess, sometimes singing like an angel, sometimes playing like Orpheus: behold! the sorrow of this world once amiss hath bereaved me of all.

It is not difficult here to separate the note of the old poetry from that of the new. The first sentence, in its plangency and vehemence, looks forward to *Cynthia*: the protesting "soes" which link up the chain "so far off, so many years, so great love, so many journeys" find their rhyme and close in the knell of "all alone". But when Ralegh turns from his own state to describe his Cynthia, he cannot begin beyond a conventional description, elegance and euphuism rounded off with a sententious flourish. It was some time before he could raise the whole thing to the level of his best poem.

> Such a one did I meet, good Sir,
> Such an Angelyke face,
> Who lyke a queen, like a nymphe did appeare
> By her gate, by her grace.
>
> She hath left me here all alone,
> All allone as unknowne,
> Who somtyme did me lead with her selfe
> And me lovde as her owne.

With a mind like Ralegh's, sincerity becomes a useless conception if it implies a simple, rigidly definable set of motives for any act or attitude. The only test for the sincerity of Ralegh's acts or attitudes lies in the quality of the thing itself. Ralegh's personal attitude to Elizabeth is not a matter of importance to the student of the poetry. There is intense feeling behind *Cynthia* and *Walsingham* and it is given without distortion or refraction within the medium. The idea that a poet may not successfully combine a person and a feeling in his poetry because they are not combined outside his poetry seems in any case to be an unwarranted limitation upon the poet's own powers in his work. Perhaps it may help to quote a passage on the archetype of this sort of poetry:

I find in it an account of a particular kind of an experience: that is, of something which had actual experience (the experience of the "confession" in the modern sense) and intellectual and imaginative experience (the experience of thought and the experience of dream) as its materials: and which became a third kind...neither a "confession" nor an "indiscretion" in the modern sense: nor is it a piece of Pre-Raphaelite tapestry.[3]

Ralegh's allegory works by superimposition, not by diffusion, like Spenser's. Cynthia represents Queen Elizabeth and Elizabeth Throckmorton, and Marlowe's Bride of the Sun and Keats' Principle of Beauty, and it is no technical ingenuity, far less a convenience or a confusion, to use one symbol for all these things.

*Walsingham*, which is the poetic version of the letter
to Cecil, contains within its few stanzas the germ of
*Cynthia*. The one poem works by concentration, the
other by elaboration. The figure of toil and renuncia-
tion, the pilgrim, is kept in the background: in the
foreground are the beauty of the lady, her forsaking
of her lover because he grows old: the fickle and the
steadfast love. The lady and her fickle love are described at length: the lover has only two stanzas, one
on his forlorn state, the other on the nature of his love.
But they are the climax and catastrophe, and the
tension from one to the other runs through the poem
like an electric current between anode and cathode:

> I have loved her all my youth,
> But now ould, as you see,
> Love lykes not the falling fruit
> From the withered tree.

"Look here upon this picture and on this."

> But Love is a durable fyre
> In the mynde ever burnynge:
> Never sycke, never ould, never dead,
> From itself never turninge.

Ralegh's poetry is extraordinary by any standards,
but most extraordinary when seen in relation to his
time. *Cynthia*, as we have it, is a poem of over 500 lines,
and it deals with nothing except Ralegh's state of
mind. There is practically no external reference: the

poem is concerned only with Temper and Mood. It is pure introspection: "The Book of the Ocean's Love to Cynthia". Its nearest companion is perhaps Donne's *Anatomy of the World*. Like that poem, it has no structure in the modern sense: no argument. It works by cumulation and repetition, not by progression along a straight line. Though there are places where it is involved, I have not found it more difficult or incoherent than Donne. Ralegh has not so obviously used philosophic conceptions; but incidentally he evokes such things as the distinction between mind, soul and spirit (ll. 438–44), between substance and essence (ll. 178–9, 426–30). There are only three or four themes: the Nature of Love; Time; the beauty of Cynthia; his dejected state. Reference is made occasionally to his past service (ll. 120 ff.) or to his recall from the voyage:

To seek new worlds, for golde, for prayse, for glory,
To try desire, to try love severed farr.
When I was gone, she sent her memory,
More strong than were ten thousand shipps of warr . . .,

to the life of compliment and allegory when Elizabeth was Belphoebe, or to his jealousies and court intrigues (ll. 265–8, 269–74, 326–8). But specific detail of time and place does not often intrude, and it might be thought a feat to write with such a minimum of material and yet escape monotony were it not that in the age of *The Arcadia* and even of *Tamburlaine* monotony is an inappropriate critical term. When these poets fail, it is not because they are in the modern sense monotonous.

It is nearly useless to quote from *Cynthia*, because, as Coleridge said, each part exists chiefly "to contribute to the harmony of the whole"; as isolated detail it is not particularly impressive. The effect of the poem is a matter of "keeping".[4] Ralegh does not (as Donne would) analyse his state of mind and give an exposition of the situation. He states it, he paints it; the poem does not work by explication but like an interjection or exclamation as compared with an ordinary sentence. The effect is largely built up by images, but they are used suggestively, not descriptively. For example, in their context the two lines

> On Sestos' shore, Leander's late resort,
> Hero hath left no lamp to guyde her love,

have all the power and pathos of

> The white moon is setting ayont the white wave,
> And Time is a-setting with me O !

but it is not exactly a matter of visual imagery.

The manipulation of the plangent vowels *o* and *e* may suggest the lighting and dying of the torch and the heavy alliteration of *l*'s and *r*'s helps for the sea (as in "Its melancholy, long, withdrawing roar").[5]

89

# SIR WALTER RALEGH

But the chief reverberation comes from the common use of Hero's torch as a symbol of passion, and from the implications of former happiness in "Leander's late resort".

The images of *Cynthia* are nearly all pastoral: desolate landscapes, setting suns, brawling streams, and dying gales. It is a "winter world" blighted by Cynthia's anger and estrangement:

> From fruitful trees I gather withered leves
> And glean the broken ears with miser's hands,
> Who sometimes did enjoy the waighty sheves.
> I seek fair floures amid the brinish sands,

or

> To seek for moysture in the Arabian sands
> Is but a loss of labour and of rest....

Ralegh's winter world is the means by which he bodies forth to the senses his state of mind (compare Donne's *Twickenham Gardens*). It is not artificial in the pejorative sense because it has no relation to external facts: it works by the power which it generates.

The external scene and the state of mind, in fact all Nature, is ruled by Mutabilitie: all dissolve and melt like pictures cast on to smoke. Time is at an end for him; it is winter and twilight and "Death's long night draws on".

But Cynthia stands outside the winter world. And in parts of the poem at least, her power is a spiritual power: she is beyond human feelings of joy or pain:

> she can renew and cann create
> Greene from the ground and flowers yeven
>     out of stones,
> By virtue lasting over time and date
>
> Leaving us only woe, which like the moss,
> Having compassion of unburied bones
> Cleaves to mischance and unrepayred loss.

Time and Cynthia are sometimes opposed and sometimes yoked together, as the moon waxes and wanes and yet remains unaltered in reality. When Cynthia is fickle it is her earthly aspect that is seen, which Chapman was to embody in a separate figure, the nymph Euthymia. When Cynthia is constant she represents the Principle of Beauty (if a name must be given to that which "into words no virtue can digest").

Ralegh's workmanship is rich yet plain: vowel play and variation in tempo are still his chief instruments. There is a clear sonority in his language: the words are not clogged with associations, yet he does not affect a diction: they are the words of common speech. Practically all are monosyllabic: the movement is based on the monosyllables, at all events, and reinforces the evenness of tone, the steadiness with which Ralegh sustains his "keeping". Occasionally he will become curious and detailed:

But as a boddy violently slayne
Retayneth warmth although the spirritt be gonn...
And by a poure in nature moves agayne
Till it be layd below the fatall stone....
So my forsaken hart, my withered minde,
Widdow of all the joys it once possesst,
My hopes clean out of sight with forced wind
To kingdoms strange, to lands farr off addrest:
Alone, forsaken, frindless on the shore,
With many wounds, with death's cold pangs embraced
Writes in the dust as one that could no more,
Whom love and tyme and fortune had defaced.

(ll. 73–92.)

Here there are a variety of images blended into the picture of death: the widow is brought in by "withered", and "out of sight" leads Ralegh on to a nautical image. The body moving after its murder is not used in any analytical spirit, as Donne used it with a like procession of images (*The Second Anniversary*, ll. 9–26). The last image is not dramatic; the dying sailor hardly focusses to consciousness apart from the sentiment of forlornness he carries (the actual subject of the verb "writes" is of course "my mind"). The plainness is relieved by "defaced" with its clustered submeanings: to lay waste, to efface, to defame, to overshadow.

The form of *Cynthia* is entirely fluid, in contrast with Ralegh's earlier verse. There is a parallel to the foregoing passage in *Farewell to the Court* (a poem which is explicitly recalled elsewhere in *Cynthia*, ll. 120–4):

> My lost delights, now clean from sight of land,
> Have left me all alone in unknown wayes:
> My mind to woe, my life in fortune's hand,
> Of all which past the sorrow only stayes.

In *Cynthia*, the verse scuds before the wind; in the earlier poem it is dominated by the regular beat of the iambic. In *Cynthia* the rhymes are often broken, and the stanza form varies freely from three to five lines. Yet the final effect is not one of incoherence. The trick of enclosing arguments and images within each other, as here, gives a peculiar knottiness to the poem. They seem to lose any value in pointing a direction or acting as signposts, and gain instead a kind of static intensity.

The mood of *Cynthia* is not of course entirely uniform: there are moments of irony and moments of exultation in this winter world. But none of them become sufficiently detached from the predominant mood to assert themselves separately.

At one point Ralegh breaks out that his love is no longer allowed to hide its own shortcomings and still contribute to Cynthia's glory, though others may do so:

> It had been such, it was still for the elect,
> But I must be the example in love's storye....

> (ll. 333–4.)

93

He knows well that his error was never premeditated, and had nothing to do with his love for her. But

> I leave th'excuse, sith Judgment hath been given.
> The limbs divided, sundered and a bleeding
> Cannot complayne the sentence was unyeven....
>
> (ll. 341–3.)

It is too late now! all is over. This is consciously dramatic; it is that point in the quarrel when the lull begins, and the offended party is coaxed to capitulate by suggesting all is hopeless, thereby giving them the power of producing the solution (already in sight) as entirely their own doing.

Another piece of strategy is to chant Cynthia's divinity through several stanzas, and then upbraid her with being no goddess after all:

> Yet have these wonders want which want compassion:
> Yet hath her mind some markes of human race,
> Yet will she be a woman for a fashion....

In other words, Ralegh has seen through her, but her charms are strong enough to hold him in spite of disillusionment. Even more brilliant is the manœuvre which leads him to imply throughout that he has been deserted by Elizabeth because he is growing too old for her (she was nearly twenty years his senior). It is the gist of the magnificent passage "With youth is dead the hope of love's return" (ll. 287–98), of ll. 417–25, of the conclusion and of the fragmentary twelfth book. The idea is kept at the level of a suggestion: it is never made explicit, when its absurdity might become unavoidable.

The informing feeling of these passages, quite other than this immediate one, is a tragic lament for Time and Fate and Change. This is indeed the main subject of the poem. The love which is dependent on "forms externall" only lasts while those "sunny beawties" are in their prime (ll. 175–80). But Elizabeth's beauty is one that

> tyme ripeth not,
> Time that but works on frayle mortality...
>
> (ll. 186–7)

and his love is not affected either by time or by her estrangement:

> My love is not of time, nor bound to date.
> My hart's internall heat and living fire
>
> Would not or could be quencht with sudden showres,
> My bound respect was not confined to dayes,
> My vowed fayth not sett to ended houres.
>
> (ll. 301–5.)

This impresses by the pomp and ceremony of balanced stresses: it moves by the simplicity of the phrasing. Ralegh's success, like Marlowe's, lay in the power to combine ceremony of movement and plain-

95

ness of diction. They might be conscious of their Grand Style: they had no need to cultivate it, and their energy was not frittered on polishing the details.

The most complete statement of the nature of love comes at the end of the poem (ll. 376–449). There Ralegh rises to a kind of iterative chant, as he describes the qualities of his love, its functions and its relation to his "cause of being":

Oh love, the more my woe, to it thou art
Yeven as the moysture to each plant that growes,
Yeven as the sun unto the frosen ground,
Yeven as the sweetness to th'incarnate rose,
Yeven as the centre in each perfait rounde....

Nothing can destroy "the essential love, of no frayle parts compounded", though the joy and hope of it are ended, and the bitter recollection would be enough to destroy a love based on external fancy. Love gave him a right to claim immortality: being by nature idle, his soul was quickened only by Cynthia's virtues; and therefore in whatever degree he may err, as a man and a mortal,

Oh love, it is but vayne to say thou were,
Ages and times cannot thy poure outrun....

It is characteristic of Ralegh that after this magnificent passage, with the absolute conviction of its measured repetition, and the ardour of its exclamations, he should drop to a couple of stanzas of irony:

96

> But what of those or these or what of ought
> Of that which was or that which is, to treat?
> What I possess is but the same I sought,
> My love was false, my labours were desayte,
>
> Nor less than such they ar esteemed to bee,
> A fraud bought at the price of many woes,
> A guile whereof the profitts unto mee
> Could it be thought premeditate for those?

There is no point of talking of ὂν καὶ μὴ ὄν. He has
got what he deserved: his love was false, as Cynthia
says: that is, it played him false, he was cheated and
paid heavily. Who could doubt that a room in the
Tower was not the goal of his ambition all along?

And then as rapidly he moves to the winter world:
withered leaves, stormy seas, scattered flocks, old age,
death. And so back to his love again, which draws
him even yet:

> To God I leave it, who first gave it me,
> And I her gave, and she returned again,
> As it was hers, so let his mercies be,
> Of my last comforts, the essential mean.
> But be it so or not, th'effects are passed.
> Her love hath end. My woe must ever last.

It is the peculiar quality of *Cynthia* to be intense and
yet not concentrated: it is like somè luminous mist,
without visible shape or cohesion, but held together
by molecular tension. Ralegh's other poems are often
both intense and concentrated: but they are never,

97

like the poems of the metaphysicals, concerned with analysis. The "thought" which appears in Donne's poems, however well digested, does imply an argument: it moves from point to point; it brings together separate items, welds certain details. The "thoughtfulness" of Ralegh's poetry is of another kind: it is neither so obvious, nor, at its best, so soon exhausted. For once a poem of Donne has been apprehended, and the exhilaration of following his vivid and curious mind has been worn by familiarity, his poems are apt to fall flatter than Ralegh's less explicit verse. This is not to say that Ralegh was the more accomplished poet; only that he had the more integrated mind.

The mood of *Cynthia* is the obverse of *Tamburlaine*: it is sustained and unadulterated regret, and *Tamburlaine* is sustained and unadulterated triumph. Ralegh was not to develop beyond this stage. Though he has echoes of Marlowe's later work, as in the lines quoted about Hero and Leander, or that other which sums the mood of *Dr Faustus*:

The thought of passed times like flames of hell,

he was never to acquire Marlowe's kind of flexibility. It could only be had by more intensive practice in writing poetry than Ralegh ever gave himself. He remained an amateur: to the end he was capable of writing only under pressure either of feeling or of circumstances. His answer to Marlowe's *The Passionate Shepherd to his Love* is unworthy because he only indicated what he wanted to say, instead of saying it. "If all the world and love were young" is a good opening, but the pastoralism is dead in more senses than one.

> The flowers doe fade, and wanton fieldes
> To wayward winter reckoning yeeldes....

It serves to show how completely these conventional landscapes depended for their effectiveness upon being the vehicle for an experience which was newly and freshly felt.

His real answer was not this, but *Walsingham*, where he found the right view-point, the right eye-level as it were; not that of the prudent nymph, but the bitter pilgrim.

The active and contemplative man maintained a balance of power in Ralegh. This is reflected in his style. The active man ensured that his writing, if complex, should not be complicated: much of his work has a kind of surface smoothness, in which the strain and shift of contrary moods and impulses can be detected, but not separately; like coloured patterns blown in glass. Sometimes it has the straightforward power of a good piece of dispatch writing.[6] The result is that while Ralegh can be as complex as Donne, his complexities are not so near the surface and cannot be drawn out in the same way.

His best writing has the maturity of all his varied experiences behind it: he could gather up "all the pride, cruelty and ambition of man, and cover it over with two narrow words". But there is also an immediate energy which jets this rich material on to the page with a force which is usually only the result of naïveté and spontaneity.

# V

## MARLOWE

Neat Marlowe, bathed in the Thespian springs,
Had in him those brave translunary things
That the first poets had: his raptures were
All air and fire, which made his verses clear:
For that fine madness still he did retain
Which rightly should possess a poet's brain.

MICHAEL DRAYTON, *To his deere friend*
*Henery Reynolds Esq., of Poets and Poesy.*

Marlowe is one who gives rather than borrows light. If he did not invent blank verse in the sense of discovering it, he developed it far beyond its origin, and his sense of structure was quite as revolutionary as his versification. *Hero and Leander* is technically much nearer to modern narrative than *Venus and Adonis*.

Marlowe was not only a great poet but "not excepting Shakespeare or Chapman the most *thoughtful* and philosophic mind, though immature, among the Elizabethan dramatists".[1] And his development followed a curve very similar to Ralegh's, though since all we know of it survives in poetry, it is a far more unified and impressive achievement. He began with the same determination to explore the countries of the mind without reserve. He thought knowledge was the goal of humanity, but only because knowledge could be translated to external power, to sovereignty. Tamburlaine defied the gods: his pride was blasphemous and without bounds; he would

> resolve of rule,
> And by profession be ambitious.

In *Dr Faustus* knowledge and sovereignty are more thoroughly identified: but knowledge is recognized to be only empirical and scientific and this is no longer satisfactory. Faustus cannot solve the riddle of ὄν καὶ μὴ ὄν; throughout the play he seeks knowledge and is put off with information, or with the power to control natural forces without understanding them: "quod est, non quid est", as Ralegh said in *The Sceptic*.

Whenever he summons Mephistopheles it is to catechize him: "What is Lucifer thy Lord?...Where are you damned?...What good will my soul do thy Lord?...Where is Hell?..." He falls back upon shows and astrology only when his soul is given away and then because Mephistopheles will not answer any deeper questions.

*Faustus.*    Villain, have I not bound thee to tell me anything?

*Mephisto.*   Ay, that is not against our Kingdom. This is: Thou art damned: think thou of Hell.

Faustus is in the position of *The Sceptic*. Nothing can certainly be known as it is in itself: only the "how", never the "what". His disputes, his wanton displays of power over Nature cover disillusion: he cannot buy certainty even at the price of his soul.

But there was no retreat to orthodoxy. In the very beginning of the play that was abandoned, with Jerome's Bible, where Faustus finds some of those "Contrarieties of Scripture" that Marlowe was accused of reporting to "some great men":[2]

Stipendium peccati mors est: Ha! stipendium peccati
  mors est.
The reward of sin is death: that's hard.
Si peccasse negamus, fallimur
Et nulla est in nobis veritas.
If we say we have no sin
We deceive ourselves and there is no truth in us.
Why then belike we must sin
And so consequently die.
Ay, we must die an everlasting death.
What doctrine call you this? Che sarà, sarà,
What will be, shall be: divinity, adieu. (1.1.39–49.)

But though Faustus dismisses philosophy as "odious
and obscure" and divinity as "unpleasant, harsh,
contemptible and vile", it is of this that he would
dispute if Mephistopheles would let him. Faustus'
conjuring tricks are suspiciously like parodies of the
Miracles: the false leg and the bottle of hay may
represent the jests about Moyses and our Saviour with
which Marlowe scandalized Kyd. He does not believe
in survival (2. 1. 134–5), and in any case he dares
damnation:

    My ghost be with the old philosophers!

Faustus finally finds satisfaction, not in such knowledge as he can attain or in the control of Nature, but
in a shadow which he knows to be only a shadow,
which he describes as beginning in the remoteness of

a Cynthian empyrean, and ending in the transparent beauty of a stream:

> Oh! thou art fairer than the evening air
> Clad in the beauty of a thousand stars;
> Brighter thou art than flaming Jupiter
> When he appeared to hapless Semele;
> More lovely than the monarch of the sky
> In wanton Arethusa's azure arms;
> And none but thou shalt be my paramour!
>
> (5. 1. 120–6.)

This is a development from the method of *Cynthia*. Moreover, it can hardly be coincidence that Marlowe uses the very name in *Tamburlaine, Part II*, where he sets Christendom in the persons of the kings against the doctrine of Christianity, and they are weighed in the balance and found wanting. The kings break an oath, which they have sworn by Christ; and the Mohammedan leader cries:

> Open, thou shining veil of Cynthia,
> And make a passage from the empyreal heaven,
> That he that sits on high and never sleeps,
> Nor in one place is circumscriptible,
> But everywhere fills every continent
> With strange infusion of his sacred vigour,
> May, in his endless power and purity,
> Behold and venge this traitor's perjury!
>
> (*Tamburlaine, II*, 2. 2. 47–54.)

This is the most positive statement of the nature of God that occurs in any of Marlowe's writings: it fits perfectly with the account we have of Ralegh's views of the "great and incomprehensible God" into whom, as into an ocean, all human knowledge flowed and lost itself.[3] However, the tension in this passage between Immanence and Transcendence is more complicated than any of Ralegh's writing.

After this, the Mohammedan goes on to describe a Turkish hell in which the Christians will be tormented. They will eat of Zoacum, the flaming tree, whose apples are the heads of devils, and they shall be led through Orcus, the gulf of fire,

From pain to pain, whose change shall never end.

This victory, he considers, proves the powers of Christ,

Which here appear as full
As rays of Cynthia to the clearest sight.

But later, when Tamburlaine burns the Koran, he does it in words which recall the gospels. It is plain that Marlowe was seriously weighing Christ with Mohammed and both are rejected for "The God that sits in Heaven and none but he" (5. 1. 200–1).

In *Tamburlaine*, then, Marlowe is still too much of an iconoclast to hold steadily to his vision of the God who sits on high and never sleeps. There are two other direct and very important statements which go to show the reason; the lines dealing with the soul and its faculties, "The thirst of reign and sweetness of a crown"; and "What is Beauty, saith my sufferings, then?" (*Tamburlaine, I*, 2. 7. 12–29, and 5. 2. 97–128).

As God fills everything "with strange infusion of his sacred vigour", so the mind is naturally inclined to "aspire" and has potentially the power to include within itself the whole universe.

> Our souls, whose faculties can comprehend
> The wondrous Architecture of the world
> And measure every Planet's wandering course....

That is, as Ralegh said, the soul can image in thought what God permeates by "infusion". Reason, the highest faculty of the soul, can enclose the image of the universe as in a mirror. And philosophy expresses itself naturally in terms of science: it is Harriot's astronomy which demonstrates man's power to the fullest.[4] (Harriot was the first man in England to see the satellites of Jupiter.)

In 1587, scientific knowledge is still knowledge *par excellence* for Marlowe. He can imagine nothing higher than this: and yet our souls

> Still-climbing after knowledge infinite
> And always moving as the restless spheres,
> Will us to wear ourselves and never rest
> Until we reach that ripest fruit of all,
> That perfect bliss and sole felicity,
> The sweet fruition of an earthly crown.

# MARLOWE

Here the mind is baffled and turns on itself. The ambiguity of "still-climbing" (always climbing and climbing without progression) leaves man "perned in a gyre", moving indeed, but enclosed within the circles of the spheres. Knowledge is infinite; that is given in the straight-soaring of the "mighty line", but the movement is not cumulative and flags to "the sweet fruition of an earthly crown". In fact the whole passage about the soul and knowledge occurs as a mere parenthesis in Tamburlaine's argument to justify attacking Cosroe: it is flanked with prudential matter. This sudden drop from one level of argument to another is one of the habits which Marlowe most strikingly shares with Ralegh.[5]

"Knowledge" (which Chapman would have called Skill) was for Marlowe to be pursued and not attained, though as yet he did not clearly admit it. But Beauty was winged from the first. There is no need to quote the passage on that grace and wonder which is not to be digested into words. Beauty is instinctively attractive to the soul; and it does not raise the soul, but brings even the gods from "the fiery-spangled veil of heaven" to cottages of strowèd reeds. It is by being at once unusually sensitive to Beauty incarnate, and yet able to detach himself from it, that Tamburlaine raises his humanity to the gods, and proves that "virtue is the true nobility".

# MARLOWE

In *Dr Faustus* Marlowe had travelled far from the mood of *Tamburlaine*. The divinity of Christ is no longer in question: and if the practices of Christians are still satirized, it does not affect Christianity. What has happened is that the impulse in human minds to aspire has suddenly met and fused with its object, the downspreading from heaven of "sacred vigour". The result is symbolized kinaesthetically when Faustus describes himself still-climbing, not after knowledge, but salvation:

I would lift up my hands, but see, they hold them,
    they hold them!...
Oh I'll leap up to my God!—Who pulls me down?
See, see where Christ's blood streams i' the firmament!
One drop would save my soul, half a drop: Ah, my
    Christ!

Marlowe has shed the miracles and the literal reading of Jerome's Bible, but his doctrine that Nature teaches us to aspire has found the conclusion for the aspiring which Ralegh found. There is a passage in *The Soul* whose relationship to Marlowe deserves careful consideration:

As the fire mounteth of itself upward and is carried round with the heavens, so the soul of man is led upward somewhat by the senses, and doth many things in and out of the body without them; which shews it must have other beginning than this. Is it not a manifest argument that it cometh from God, seeing in all things it resteth not till it come to God? The mind, in searching causes, is never quiet till it come to God, and the will never is satisfied with any good till it come to the immortal goodness.[6]

This might be taken for the inverted text of *Dr Faustus*: for Faustus reaches certainty in his damnation. God is defined for him by exclusion, Heaven is known by the knowledge of its opposite state: grace and damnation are polarized.

All places shall be Hell that is not Heaven.

(2. 1. 127.)

This is far enough from orthodoxy: and the fact that Marlowe's doctrine might not be unacceptable to a modern mind should not obscure the fact that to an Elizabethan it would be heretical and blasphemous. Nor does it seem likely that his interest in conjuring and necromancy was altogether detached from religious speculation. The school evidently read Hermes and they used that Heraclitean image of fire and of flame which has in all ages symbolized states of trance and of "rapture".

Both Marlowe and Chapman, in fact, use the technical term often: but to describe their states and faculties they use the image of the flame, of the sun and of the moon.

Fieriness at its simplest signifies energy of living—*vis vivida animi*. Tamburlaine's looks are fiery (1. 2. 56 and 157) and especially his eyes, whose

> fiery circles bear encompassed
> A heaven of heavenly bodies in their spheres
> That guides his steps and action to the throne....
> (2. 1. 15–17.)

In his own eyes Tamburlaine carries his fate, instead of it being written in the stars. As he says himself, he controls the Fates in virtue of his pure energy "lift upward and divine". He passes through his career in "sunbright armour" of victory and with the fiery comet of revenge above his hosts (4. 2. 52–5), to his death scene, where his body withers, as

> not of force enough
> To hold the fiery spirit it contains.

It has been pointed out that this scene is modelled on the *Hercules Furens*, and that Tamburlaine assumes the god by an ordeal of fire, as Hercules on Mount Oeta. When Zenocrate dies he begins to aspire:

> Batter the shining palace of the sun,
> And shiver all the starry firmament,

and by bringing in Zenocrate's coffin at his death he recalls this. His "burning agony" is a purification and, though earth loses its fruit,

Heaven has consumed his choicest living fire.
(Part II, 5. 3. 251.)

But Tamburlaine is always more than man. "He rides in golden armour like the Sun." The sun is the symbol of all energy in the active life, of all external power, and of dominion. Tamburlaine's chariot is the chariot of the sun, in which he sits, "the chiefest lamp of all the earth", after his "rising in the East" (4. 2. 37), and when he is drawn by the conquered kings he tells them that they are more honoured than

The horse that guide the golden eye of Heaven
And blow the morning from their nosterils,
Making their fiery gait above the clouds.
(Part II, 4. 3. 7–9.)

Through Samarcanda he goes like the son of Jove in his chariot gilt with fire (4. 3. 125–30), and when he resigns his chariot to his son it is

As precious
As that which Clymene's brainsick son did guide.
(Part II, 5. 3. 230–1.)

As Tamburlaine symbolizes the sun of the active life, Zenocrate is Cynthia or the Contemplative

Power. Her looks clear the air with crystal and, when she dies (2. 4), "black is the beauty of the brightest day". Olympia also symbolizes this power, controlling the active energy of Theridamus:

> Olympia, pity him in whom thy looks
> Have greater operation and more force
> Than Cynthia's in the watery wilderness.
>
> (Part II, 4. 2. 28–30.)

As the sun tempers the earth with heat, and produces all sensible living things, so Zenocrate tempers the living spirits of men; and she gives light to the sun. She also gives light to the moon, the planets and the meteors (Part I, 5. 2). She is called the "world's fair eye" and Tamburlaine is also called "the eye of heaven".[7] (Cf. *Dr Faustus*, 5. 2. 142.) He is more majestic than the light from

> The shining bower where Cynthia sits
> Like lovely Thetis in a crystal robe.
>
> (Part II, 3. 4. 50–1.)

There is a widely spread mystical image that man has two eyes: with one he looks into time and with the other into eternity.[8] In Marlowe, Tamburlaine the sun-god symbolizes that eye of heaven which is turned into time; and Zenocrate, the moon-goddess, symbolizes the eye which is turned towards eternity. That is why Tamburlaine wears garments of red and of gold,[9] and why Zenocrate wears white and pearly colour:[10] and yet why in the end Tamburlaine hopes for the spiritual sight to "pierce the coffin and the sheet of gold" and so regain his lost Zenocrate (5. 3. 225–7):

> Zenocrate, lovelier than love of Jove,
> Brighter than is the silver Rhodope,
> Fairer than whitest snow on Scythian hills...
> With milk-white harts upon an ivory sled
> Thou shalt be drawn amid the frozen pools,
> And scale the icy mountains' lofty tops.
>
> (Part I, 1. 2. 87–9, 98–100.)

This might be compared with Shelley's or Yeats' moon imagery. During Tamburlaine's triumphs, Zenocrate always realizes the transitory glory of "slippery crowns". She does not seek the power which she is given. When she dies, she recognizes that it is only to "wane with enforced and necessary change": she is as potent in death as in life.

One of the more important words is "crystal".[11] It gives the quality of sensuous beauty as it is in *Tamburlaine*; clear, yet remote. It is associated with the sight of the sun and moon seen through water, which, taken in conjunction with the lines describing Helen of Troy in *Dr Faustus*, suggests that all the power of *Tamburlaine* is only a transparent veil for a power which is not physical:[12]

> As looks the Sun through Nilus' flowing stream,
> Or when the morning holds him in her arms,
> So looks my lordly love, fair Tamburlaine....
>
> (Part I, 3. 2. 47–9.)

Whether Marlowe and the School of Night used the crystal we cannot tell. The god revealing himself to man as the sun reflected in water is to be found in Eckhardt.

The translucent glory of *Tamburlaine* and the winter world of *Cynthia* stand in the same relation to each other as *The Passionate Shepherd to his Love* and *The Answer*. Both are kept crisp with irony; both depend on the "keeping" and on being removed as far as possible from the everyday world, while achieving their effects largely through *unfocussed* sensuous description. Both are built on the long soaring sentence which incloses within itself a whole argument.

Marlowe's idea of the heroic soul has extreme simplicity and unbounded appetite, so that...after one subordinate clause has opened out of another with inalterable energy, it can still roar at the close with the same directness as in the opening line. Thus the lack of variety in his rhythm is in itself a device of some rhythmical subtlety....That a conditional clause should have been held back through all these successive lightnings of poetry, that after their achievement it should still be present with the same conviction *and resolution*, is itself a statement of heroic character.[13]

This might serve as a description of *Cynthia*, e.g. the lines quoted on p. 92 ("So my forsaken hart"). Allowing for the differences between lyric and dramatic writing, and that Ralegh's poem was the culmination of his work while Marlowe's marked his beginning, the two poets have as much in common as such individualists might ever hope for.

*Tamburlaine* and *Dr Faustus* are indebted to the School of Night in more specific ways. The number of astronomical references is generally commented on;[14] and Marlowe is surprisingly accurate. It is more important to see how naturally and inevitably they blend into the other matters he is dealing with: by how many ways they are linked up with philosophy and psychology, and how accessible they are for ordinary descriptive work. They are the backbone of the passage on the Soul and of "What is Beauty?"; and at least they contribute to the effect of "Open, thou shining veil of Cynthia". Faustus engages in long discussions of astronomy (e.g. 2. 2. 33–68). There are at least a dozen references of importance in *Tamburlaine*, as a glance at the index in Miss Ellis-Fermor's edition will show, especially at the deaths of Zenocrate and Tamburlaine. In his later plays

Marlowe's interest in astronomy seems to have declined.

*Tamburlaine* also shows more than a nodding acquaintance with geography and gunnery. Miss Ethel Seaton proved conclusively that Marlowe had studied the latest maps with attention and followed them accurately. *A priori*, there seems no reason for such an interest in the technical side of the subject; he himself had never been beyond France at most or fought at any time, but as a member of Ralegh's and Keymis' circle he would have been bound to have heard a good deal of navigation and artillery.

Ralegh's explorations can be felt behind the aspirations of both Tamburlaine and Faustus. When at his death the former laments for South America unconquered,

> All the golden mines,
> Inestimable drugs and precious stones,

or when he talks of

> Rocks of pearl that shine as bright
> As all the lamps that beautify the sky,
>
> (5. 3. 151–2, 156–7)

he is probably drawing directly upon the conversations of Harriot and Keymis and Ralegh. When

# MARLOWE

Faustus sees his earliest vision of power, it is in terms of Guiana and the *Madre de Dios*:

> As Indian Moors obey their Spanish lords,
> So shall the spirits of every element
> Be always serviceable to us three....
> From Venice shall they drag huge argosies
> And from America the golden fleece
> That yearly stuffs old Philip's treasury.
> (Dr Faustus, 1. 1. 122–4, 131–3.)

Such passages might have been inspired by *The Discovery of Guiana*, did not chronology forbid: nevertheless, Ralegh's talk must always have turned in this direction: his house was open to sailors, and the Gilberts were adventuring. "Marlowe's map", Marlowe's language, and Marlowe's exuberance confirm that behind the splendour of *Tamburlaine* were thoughts of

> A...beautiful country...lively prospects...hils so raised here and there over the valleys, the river winding into divers branches, the planes adioyning without bank or stubble, all fair greene grasse, the ground of hard sand easie to march on, either for horse or foote, the deere crossing in everie path, the brides towards the evening singing on every tree, with a thousand severall tunes, cranes and herons of white, crimson and carnation, pearching in the river's side, the air fresh with a gentle Easterly winde, and every

stone that we stouped to take up, promised either golde or silver by his complexion.

*(Discovery of Guiana, Works,* vol. VIII, p. 442.)

Ralegh kept that spirit through sickness and imprisonment; with Marlowe it did not last beyond five-and-twenty.

But in *Dr Faustus* Marlowe had developed beyond the point where he could absorb much from the School of Night. They had supplied him with the new material: as a poet he had outgrown them. The flexibility of his line, the litheness of his sentence structure and the colloquial tone of much of the verse are far removed from *Tamburlaine*—so far that even Chapman never caught up with Marlowe in this respect: his verse derives from *Tamburlaine*, and not from the later plays.

That Chapman should have been drawn to finish *Hero and Leander* is one of the most surprising results of the friendships of the School of Night. Marlowe had riddled all his most cherished doctrine as effectively as Berowne was to do: indeed the poem was in flat revolt against all the School of Night, and Marlowe seems to have served them as Ralegh served Machiavelli. Their doctrine is quoted and their writings recalled for the sole purpose of demolishing their credit. It is Marlowe in his mood of greatest devilment who compares Hero diving into the bed-clothes to

> Chaste Diana when Actaeon spied her,

and who quotes the respectable Warner,

> Seeming not won, yet was she won at length.
> In such wars women use but half their strength,[15]

who opens the amorous war between Hero and Leander by comparing Hero to Cynthia (First Sestiad, ll. 107–12) and the debate with "a periphrasis of Night":

> The air with sparks of living fire was spangled;
> And Night deep-drenched in misty Acheron
> Heaved up her head and half the world upon
> Breathed darkness forth (dark night is Cupid's day).
> > (*Ibid.* ll. 188–91.)

The debate between the lovers is conducted by quotations from Aristotle, but they are those which had already been used by Warner in *Albion's England*.

Marlowe's combination of exuberance and irony comes out most plainly in his treatment of Hero. He enjoys her efforts to escape; "like a planet moving several ways" she struggles to avoid Leander, but her prayers are beaten down by Cupid, and in deliberate

caricature he is shown as an infant Tamburlaine
threatening a Damascene Virgin:

> Cupid beats down her prayers with his wings,
> Her vows about the empty air he flings;
> All deep enraged, his sinewy bow he bent
> And shot a shaft that burning from him went.
>
> (First Sestiad, ll. 369–72.)

Marlowe triumphantly identifies himself with the
gods as against the mortals: but the gods are all
disreputable; in the crystal pavement of the temple
which reflects the firmament they are

> Committing heady incests, riots, rapes...
> Jove...for his love Europa bellowing loud
> And tumbling with the rainbow in a cloud.
>
> (First Sestiad, ll. 141–50.)

*Hero and Leander* is written in a mood of exultant
comedy, in which all pretensions to chastity are be-
mocked. Even the toothless Destinies have fallen in
love with Mercury, and for his sake they will reverse
the order of the whole world and restore the golden
age. The farce of their unrequited passion is only a
stronger version of Neptune's doting love for Leander,
or the attitude of the general population of Sestos
towards Hero and that of Abydos towards Leander.
Marlowe approves of passion, but he is not at all implicated: on the contrary he is emphatically mundane,

unheroic (not mock-heroic, of course); and, most
important of all, exaggerating and revelling in the
limitations of ordinary human nature, instead of
trying to transcend them.

> So ran the people forth to gaze upon her,
> And all that saw her were enamoured on her...
> ...(All) wait the sentence of her scornful eyes.
> He whom she favours, lives: the other dies.
> There might you see one sigh, another rage,
> And some, their violent passions assuage,
> Compile sharp satires: but, alas, too late....
>
> (First Sestiad, ll. 117–27.)

The cheerful summing up caps the jaunty double
rhymes: the description is in a vein of mockery comparable to that of Ralegh's verses to his son. Marlowe
is both ironically detached and sympathetically identified with the lovers. He accepts and rejoices in the
power of Nature to overwhelm the rational and
intellectual powers. Even at the end Hero deceives
herself (or half of herself):

> In her own mind she thought herself secure,
> O'ercast with dim and *darksome* coverture.[16]
>
> (Second Sestiad, ll. 265–6.)

It is well that wit should be used sometimes to
baffle wit, that the world should befool itself, that
Hero should know, but not admit, what she is doing:
it makes for richness of living, as Aristotle saw:[17]

She trembling strove: this strife of hers (like that
Which made the world) another world begat
Of unknown joy.      (Second Sestiad, ll. 291-3.)

It is Shakespeare's doctrine of submission to the flux
of living as the surest method of controlling it:

Light, seeking light, doth light of light beguile.
                    (*Love's Labour's Lost*, 1. 1. 77.)

Marlowe has proved it so in poetry, as far as he
himself is concerned. *Hero and Leander* has more
"body" in its language, a control of different levels of
experience, and a power to interanimate the different
levels; above all, it points in the direction in which the
language of poetry was moving. It is not only an
advance, but an advance in the main direction:
towards the poetry of Shakespeare and Donne.

# VI

## CHAPMAN

Like some watcher of the skies,
When a new planet swims into his ken.

JOHN KEATS, *Sonnet on first looking*
*into Chapman's Homer.*

It is not merely the heavy and convulsive movement of
the broken and jarring sentences, the hurried and broken-
winded rhetoric that seems to wheeze and pant at every
painful step, the incessant byplay of incongruous di-
gressions and impenetrable allusions that make the first
reading of these poems as tough and tedious a task for
the mind as oakum picking or stone breaking can be for
the body. Worse than all this is the want of any perceptible
centre towards which these tangled and ravelled lines of
thought may seem at least to converge.

ALGERNON SWINBURNE, *An Essay on George Chapman.*

Chapman has to contend with a bad reputation, particularly in his non-dramatic poetry. His connection with the School of Night is not too easy to determine: but it is sufficiently clear to elucidate, in part at least, that baffling poem, *The Shadow of Night*, and to suggest a technique of reading which may be helpful for the rest of his poetry. The explanation briefly is that *The Shadow of Night* is an allegory, which, like *Cynthia*, has a general and a particular application. It contains two hymns, *Hymnus in Noctem* and *Hymnus in Cynthiam*: the first laments the injustice of the world and the neglect of virtue and describes Ralegh's dejected state. The second celebrates the triumphs and glories of Cynthia, by whom Chapman states he means both the Contemplative Power and Queen Elizabeth.[1] Cynthia, in fact, is the same symbol for Chapman as for Ralegh.

*The Shadow of Night* was entered for publication on December 31st, 1593. It was published early the next year. If Chapman were trying to help Ralegh to regain Elizabeth's favour, this was a little late: the poem might have been useful a year earlier. And if it had provoked Shakespeare in *Love's Labour's Lost* to parody certain lines, it must have been written then; for the first production of the play almost certainly falls in the winter of 1593–4; the evidence may be found summarized in the Cambridge *New Shakespeare,* pp. 126–7.

The poem was therefore satirized from manuscript, before it appeared in print, for the benefit of Essex' coterie. It is likely that in this case Chapman would alter those parts which had been the readiest targets: he would not court a larger ridicule by publishing them as they stood. This would have meant revision of the first hymn: Shakespeare had attacked Ralegh, naturally not Elizabeth. So it happens that the political allegory is not nearly so prominent in the first half as in the second, and that the first hymn, *Hymnus in Noctem,* has nearly twice as many heroic similes as the second thrust into the text to replace the excised passages. The quite exceptional shapelessness of these poems is therefore partly due to hasty revision.

But the "strangeness" of the poem is also a matter of "doctrine", and the doctrine is that of the School of Night at its most esoteric and transcendental. The tendency of the school was reinforced by Chapman's natural bent. For his separation from the crowd was not, as it was with Ralegh and Marlowe, a matter of superiority, but really of separation, of incompatibility. He recognized no varied levels of discourse: he had none of Ralegh's flexibility of mind, or Marlowe's liveliness of temper.

Hence, though his poems are much more directly connected with the theories of the school than Marlowe's are, he has not the latter's temperamental affinities with Ralegh, and the connection between the poet and the courtier seems to have been a slight one. Chapman was apparently introduced by Matthew Roydon, and perhaps he attempted to gain the place that Spenser had held with Ralegh. He seems to have established friendships with Harriot, Hughes and Keymis, but not with their patron. His efforts to do so, if they were as clumsy as those which he later used to gain the interest of the Earl of Somerset, would be more likely to antagonize than to soften Ralegh.

At this period, Chapman was very undeveloped as a writer. His earliest plays are mere hackwork, and he seems to have looked on them as such and reserved his energies for his lyric poetry. Though his earliest lyric has generally been received in the spirit of Swinburne, as a kind of unnatural birth, yet it has more than the personal value, which it undoubtedly possessed for Chapman, of offering a free exercising ground for his personal technique. It may be felt that Chapman, like Blake in the Prophetic Books, does not justify his obscurity as a necessary condition of successful poetry: but it may be conceded, as it generally is to Blake, that his obscurity was not the result of dishonesty or affectation.

# CHAPMAN

Against this, there might be urged those much misunderstood and misread documents, his dedicatory letters. But these must not be taken in a void. They are a defence of the school as well as himself, and a protest against Shakespeare's ridicule of study, in which that "passion-driven man" had taken it upon himself to be "judgment's butcher".

Chapman mentions Derby, Northumberland and Carey. "Their high deserving virtues may cause me hereafter strike that fire out of darkness which the brightest Day shall envy for beauty." The defiant tone of this manifesto is not unprovoked, if it comes in reply to *Love's Labour's Lost*, and in defence of a poem already ridiculed. The rude multitude is challenged not to understand the poem, but to like it: for Knowledge and Skill require Herculean labours in their search, and Chapman has undergone them gladly. (Skill was his name for any specialized study: in the poem he speaks of the Court of Skill, that is, the School of Night.) The preface should be read as a general defence of learning, in reply to Berowne:[2]

It is an exceeding rapture of delight in the deep search of knowledge (none knoweth better than thyself, sweet Matthew) that maketh man manfully to endure the extremes incident to that Herculean labour: from flint must the Gorgonean fount be smitten.

All direct mention of Ralegh is excluded, and

CHAPMAN

though Chapman addresses the circle, he does not approach Ralegh personally till two years later, in the *De Guiana Carmen Epicum*. It seems as if his attempt to play Spenser's rôle had not succeeded with Ralegh: and if he had offered such a ready means of attack to the other party, this is quite understandable.

The poem therefore reflects Ralegh's views rather than his circumstances. Chapman recalls *The Sceptic* when he describes the intimate connection between physical constitution and temperament, and how they vary proportionably. If man behaves like a beast, he should look like a beast, according to Chapman. He is also like Ralegh in his separation of Contemplation from Reason, which has little share in his religious experiences. It is "in sleep" that his "waking soul" is loosed to see visions of good and evil. The material world seems to him shadowy and mutable as it did to Ralegh, and material happiness the shadow of a shadow:

If these be dreams, even so are all things else
That walk their rounds by heavenly sentinels...
If these seem likewise vain, or nothing are,
Vain things, or nothing, come to virtue's share:
For nothing more than dreams with us she finds....

But Ralegh had at least given Reason more of a trial than Chapman did, before he recognized its inadequacy. Chapman looked on his "learning" as something to be endured for the sake of the raptures and ecstasies it brought him. Reason was not merely useless but encumbering.

As his rejection of Reason is more uncompromising than Ralegh's, so his attitude toward the material world is not a negative one, but full of loathing and disgust. Ralegh's acute consciousness of death does not make him see all life as

This load of life in life, this fleshly stone,
This bond and bundle of corruption—
This breathing sepulchre—this sponge of grief—
This smiling enemy—this household thief—
This glass of air, broken with less than breath—
This slave bound face to face with Death till death. . . .

Ralegh was both active and contemplative by turns: Chapman was altogether a contemplative. His attitude towards women, for instance, was one of cynicism covering mistrust. It was ill calculated to help Ralegh. In 1593 it was not tactful to observe that
                                thy sacred train,
        Thrice mighty Cynthia, should be frozen dead
        To all the lawless flames of Cupid's godhead.

Chapman's cult of chastity and its incompatibility with Ralegh was Shakespeare's chance, and he seized it.

# CHAPMAN

Chapman seems to have laid a very different emphasis on his studies from the other members of the school. Though he used philosophical terminology, he was very inaccurate: and he always spoke of the subject with a deference which does not suggest familiarity. Antony à Wood says that he was not good at philosophy and logic: it is still more difficult to imagine him taking any interest in mathematics. On the other hand he was deeply influenced by the Hermetic writings and perhaps by Plotinus, as Miss Janet Spens has shown.[3] Chapman had a gnomic rather than a speculative mind, without either the intellectual powers of Ralegh and Marlowe, or their capacity for detachment and self-criticism. He could not manipulate either his mind or the contents of his mind with the same ease. He had of course far less experience of the world than Marlowe, infinitely less than Ralegh. He withdrew from it to wrestle with spiritual problems, and tried to ignore the common needs of life, complaining bitterly to Harriot about the necessity of paying any attention to the body,[4] instead of "aspiring ...the whole sphere of Fire".

In his writing he betrays the habits of a recluse. He has private symbols and private uses of words, and it puzzles and antagonizes him that other people do not grasp his codes. If they did not follow his very unexpected application of myth in *Andromeda Liberata*,

CHAPMAN

or his defence of the Massacre of St Bartholomew from
general principles, Chapman concluded it was their
fault, not his.

In *The Shadow of Night* he used one of his favourite
symbols: his mottoes nearly always have some reference to the night and his verses to Nenna were
signed "Ex tenebris". It seems to have signified both
his dejected states, his "nights of sorrow"[5] and his
trances or "raptures".

Chapman's power lay in his capacity to treat a
general subject with the poignancy of the immediate
and the particular, and in that way it resembled
Ralegh's. But he did not take a simple, public con-
vention to express it, as Ralegh took the pastoral: he
evolved a private and cumbrous one. The *Hymnus in
Noctem* is a lament for all the cruelty, injustice and
corruption of things as they are. His own misfortunes
(and Ralegh's) are only examples of the general plight.
He would raise his soul

That in my tortures she all earth's may sing.

Chapman sees the world reduced to a second Chaos.
The stepdame Night-of-Mind broods over it, and
breeds "worlds of confusion". What appals Chapman
is the blind unspiritual state of most men, who live
grossly as beasts, thinking only of their lusts. They are
"transformed to Calydonian boars" and use their

reason only for self-love. Like Timon of Athens, he thinks the commonwealth is become a forest of beasts.[6]

Harpies and centaurs and such-like creatures are the poet's symbols of what man has become: if they bear the minds of beasts, their bodies should correspond. Man must earn his humanity: or self-love will lead him on the one hand to pride and ambition, and on the other to luxury or avarice.

Chapman calls upon the Eumenides to execute judgment on the world and on Hercules to help them:

> Fall, Hercules, from heaven in tempests hurled,
> And cleanse the beastly stable of this world...;

but his only settled hope seems to be a retreat into contemplation. One who is

> ennobled with the deathless love
> Of things eternal, dignified above,

would wait till the Night "beats in the fowls and beasts to Somnus' lodgings". When his own baser desires are thus laid asleep he would summon "all living spirits" to

> Aspire th'extraction and the quintessence
> Of all the joys in earth's circumference.

They are to compose poems which, in "a body figured to your virtues' ruth", may show the senses of common men the chaotic state of this world. He

CHAPMAN

condemns the senses, and the bodily eye, which, un-
heeding the "second light", "enflames the heart and
learns the sense abuse". Instead, he exalts the night
which, in its visions and dreams, reproduces in greater
beauty all the visions of the day. He ends with the
pageant of Night's Triumph, in whose train comes
Cynthia as an enchantress:

Music and mood she loves, but love she hates,
(As curious ladies do, their public cates).

Night plays a double rôle. It signifies sorrow, dejection and spiritual uncertainty and in this sense
corresponds with Ralegh's "winter world". But it is
also the necessary state for the act of contemplation,
the appearance of Cynthia: in this sense it is the central
image in many mystical writings, from those of
Dionysius the Areopagite to St John of the Cross.

The first hymn alone would show that Chapman's
attitude to men in general was not that of Ralegh and
Marlowe. He was acutely and constantly aware that
pride was a deadly sin, and that man should "fall
worm-like on the ground" before his creator. Chapman's own pride is based on a discrimination between
"l'homme sensuel moyen" and the "superior man".
He was very nice in his choice of friends, as Antony à
Wood tells us, and as his poem *On Friendship* might
show. It was not the ignorance, but the brutality of

136

CHAPMAN

the mob which he disliked: and he disliked these
qualities wherever they showed.

For its first half the *Hymnus in Cynthiam* is addressed
directly to the queen. There are unmistakable references to her illness of 1593. England is referred to as
"Ephesia", Diana's city: and the Court is her temple.

He describes her first of all as ageless, and Time as
a moth dazzled by her beauty:

> Ascend thy chariot and make earth admire
> Thy old swift changes made a young fixed prime.
> O, let thy beauty scorch the wings of Time
> That fluttering he may fall before thine eyes,
> And beat himself to death before he rise.
>
> (ll. 16–20.)

As chastity was supposed to confer immortality
upon the gods, so Elizabeth's chastity should preserve
her: if she is once eclipsed, not all the ceremonies of
antiquity can "further her recall". There would be
warfare as deadly as the field of Cannae if "interposed
earth" (a typical conceit) obscured Cynthia's light:

> So, gracious Cynthia, in that sable day
> When interposed earth takes thee away,
> (Our sacred chief and sovereign general)
> As crimson a retreat and steep a fall
> We fear to suffer from this peace and height
> Whose thankless sweet now cloys us with receipt.
>
> (ll. 58–63.)

137

The whole state of England, which depends on her, and whose "humours" she sways and governs, would suffer violent change:

> Ephesia's state will be
> But spoil with foreign grace, and change with thee.
> The pureness of thy never-tainted life,
> Scorning the subject title of a wife....
> Commits most willing rapes on all our hearts
> And make us tremble lest thy sovereign parts
> (The whole preservers of our happiness)
> Should yield to change, eclipse or heaviness.
>
> (ll. 93–6, 103–6.)

He goes on to describe at length the dejected state of all who oppose her and the happy state of those she favours. The virtuous-tempered mind resembles Cynthia in this, that it can subdue the forms of external things to itself (cf. p. 91):

> She is the great enchantress that commands
> Spirits of every region, seas and lands....
> A perfect type of thy Almighty state.
>
> (ll. 135–9.)

Therefore he intends to sing the praises of Cynthia both as the "sovereign kind" (Elizabeth) and as the power of the Contemplative Intellect. This is an argument to ravish an earthly soul: and all who are not capable of such ravishment are warned to keep aloof, for it is necessary "to sever mounting spirits from the senses". This warning refers to the symbolic narrative which immediately follows, and which takes up the greater part of the poem.

Cynthia descends to the earth and first builds herself a palace, "Pax Imperii named", where she sits and rules in state. She fashions out of a meteor a nymph named Euthymia or Concord: and from flowers and mists she makes hunters and hounds. The nymph can turn herself into the shape of any beast, and so first as a panther she is chased by the hunters and by Cynthia, but leads them into a dreadful thicket, where those who opposed Cynthia have been imprisoned. The hunters and hounds are repelled by the horrible sights of these monsters, and the nymph escapes. She now becomes a boar, and flees to a beautiful island: the hunt follows, and she leads them through mansions, gardens and groves which they lay utterly waste. But by now it is night, and Cynthia's creations all turn to mists and vapours: she mounts her chariot "and leaves us miserable creatures here".

Euthymia is spiritual Joy.[7] As a beast she represents the earthly and sensuous embodiments of joy pursued by unspiritual man. The panther is Pride, and the boar Lust.[8] The island palace is a kind of Bower of Bliss, full of deceiving "pied shows", and the hunters who pursue her there are mounted on beasts of various kinds. They are thus not completely identified with the beast, as in the legend of Circe, nor is Euthymia: for she has rainbow wings, which are bound up by Cynthia before she is sent to "bid the base to all affection". ("Affection" signifying "desire", Chapman's usual sense.)

The Shadowy Hunting is a recognized symbol for the pursuit of earthly desire. It is (to take a modern example) one of the recurrent symbols of Yeats:

Why are you calling, white deer with no horns?
I have been changed to a hound with one red ear....

Round the animals of this hunt there can be felt half-focussed significances, and half-remembered legends.

For it is only by ancient symbols, by symbols that have numberless meanings besides the one or two the writer lays emphasis on, or the half-score he knows of, that any highly subjective art can escape from the barrenness and shallowness of a too conscious arrangement into the abundance and depth of nature.[9]

The imagery of these poems is derived partly from Seneca (as in the description of Night in the first hymn, ll. 270–87), partly from older and savager sources, and partly from cram-books like Conti's. But even when he uses the classical deities, Chapman turns them into more monstrous and indeterminate forms than those of the Olympic hierarchy. Hecate, the enchantress with viper's hairs, the hounds that pursued Actaeon, "grim Melampus with the Ethiop's feet, white Leucon and all-eating Pamphagus" and the rest are portentous and shadowy.

At the same time they carry a political significance which turns the hunt into Elizabeth's war with Spain (there is a long simile taken from the fighting in the Low Countries). This, however, is only of subsidiary interest: it will obtrude for a few lines and then die away, like Spenser's politics in *The Faerie Queene*.

These hymns show that the use of symbolism was not without dangers for one of Chapman's analytic and introspective temper. (In this respect he was ahead of Marlowe and anticipating Donne.) Such preoccupation with the detail of personal feelings as that of Chapman demanded a new mode, explicit rather than implicit. Symbolism could become cumbrous, as Chapman was himself later to acknowledge, unless it fitted in with his subject, as it did in *De Guiana Carmen Epicum*.

This poem shows him at his best. He had a simple heroic subject, his blood was fired, and he could write consistently and without the anxious deliberation which clogged *The Shadow of Night*: he elaborated only when naturally led to it by the subject, for example when Ralegh, wielding an "Eliza-consecrated sword", is described in a simile which he perhaps provided in the first place:

## CHAPMAN

O how most like
Art thou, heroic author of this act,
To this wronged soul of Nature: that sustain'st
Pain, charge and peril for thy country's good,
And she, much like a body marred with surfeits,
Feels not....

Here Ralegh is the soul of England: and England's
disregard of him is like the corruption of natural
gifts by perverted senses. The disinterested nature of
Ralegh's interest in colonization (which he perhaps
overstressed, though it deserved stressing) exactly
fitted Chapman's anti-materialism. He eulogized the
gentlemen who risked their lives, "You that know death
lives where power lives unus'd". They might, incidentally, win gold ("a wonder, virtue rich!"), but
their glory was that they "refine their flesh to Fire"
so that in them "the tract of heaven in morn-like glory
opens". The expedition was a spiritual achievement
of Tamburlaine's kind; since those who joined refused
to endure "the prison'd life of beasts":

You that herein renounce the course of earth
And lift your eyes for guidance to the stars—

(a lovely conceit which remodels the lines from the
*Hymnus in Noctem*:

Sweet Peace's richest crown is made of stars,
Most certain guides of honour'd mariners.

(ll. 374–5)).

The poem ends with a vision of Ralegh's new colony:

Th'industrious knight, the soul of this exploit...
That is espoused for virtue to his love

passes down to his "argolian fleet", where round about "his bating colours English valour swarms" and they sail to the fabulous land of plenty.

The subject gave Chapman all he needed: a heroic enterprise. He was always at his best when carried off by physical excitement or stress, in descriptions of fights, storms, shipwrecks. That the most studious and retiring of the school should be the only one to celebrate its practical achievements in verse is a proof of its essential homogeneity.

The poem to Harriot also shows Chapman in a generous enthusiasm. He begins with an outcry against the senses:

traitors born
To their own crown, their souls: betray'd to scorn
By their base flesh's frailties....[10]

It is the body's needs which oblige men to make shameful alliances with the mammon of unrighteousness:

and our sleights
Must bear the form of fools or parasites!

It is more than a little significant that this should precede a poem dedicated to the Earl of Essex. If

143

Chapman were to seek the patronage of that fascinating but hare-brained young man, loved by the mob whom Chapman detested, he might have been driven to it by poverty. Chapman seems always to have been desperately poor: in 1598 Ralegh was oblivious of everything that was not "towards the sunset", and his hungry poet may have "set the proud full sail of his great verse" towards Essex and Southampton. This was against his principles, as well as his inclinations; and to Harriot he makes his dejection plain.

Chapman is not happy about his poetry. He is painfully conscious of the constriction of his mind, the involutions which only the "organ" of a telescope could pierce:

O had your perfect eyes organs to pierce
Into that chaos whence this stifled verse
By violence breaks: where glow-worm like doth shine
In nights of sorrow, this hid soul of mine;
And how her genuine Form struggles for birth
Under the claws of this foul panther earth:
That under all these forms you should discern
My love to you in my desire to learn.

"Struggles" is the keyword of this passage: Chapman is writhing under his own apparatus of symbols, by which he tries to order his experiences and body them forth to sense. He praises Harriot as a philosopher, and apologizes for offering poetry to so grave a student: but pleads that poetry is the means of discovering philosophy to the worldly.[11] Harriot may therefore "approve the traduction" and

> besides this
> Excuse my thoughts, as bent to others' aims.

The poem deserves study. It shows the place held by learning in Chapman's mind. He insists on its immediate relation to daily living, its fruitfulness,

> Holding all learning but an art to live well.[12]

Chapman's own difficulty in relating his learning to daily living lay in his isolation from the world. He seemed quite unable to find common ground between his spiritual states and the daily habits of life. The age gave him no help. Hence the unavoidable eccentricities of expression. His monstrous personifications, for instance, have no reference to the concrete: they are not embodiments: it would be impossible to visualize them.

Chapman had a much stronger feeling for analogies and relationships than for specific objects. Hence his love of multi-symbolic myth and his elaboration of the intrigue in his comedies. He looked much harder at the connection between things than at the things themselves. This makes him so blind to everything but the verbal link in words, as in his puns: he uses the

# CHAPMAN

words as if they were counters, without any consideration of their reverberations. The danger of Andromeda
enchained is described as if by Launce:

And now comes roaring to the Tied the Tide.[13]

It explains why his most successful imagery is generally
kinaesthetic. His imagery of fire and flame is more
often of this sort than visual. In the poem to Harriot
he uses a volcanic image:

flames
Of my pressed soul break forth to their own show;

and in *Bussy D'Ambois* it is the wheeling movement of
the Dark Sun that gives vigour to Bussy's invocation:

Terror of darkness! O thou king of flames
That with thy music-footed horse dost strike
The clear light out of crystal on dark earth,
And hurl'st instructive fire about the world,
Wake, wake the drowsy and enchanted night
That sleeps with dead eyes in this heavy riddle!

Chapman's fire has not the clarity of Marlowe's:
it is torn and spasmodic, "a torch born in the wind".
But it is under the same image of fire that he describes
his own states of rapture and inspiration, and that he
himself conjures Marlowe's spirit to help him in the
finishing of *Hero and Leander*. (That invocation is no
ornamental flourish: Chapman believed firmly in

146

# CHAPMAN

inspiration and has described one occasion on which
he was inspired by Homer.) [14]

> Then ho, most strangely-intellectual fire
> That, proper to my soul, hast power t'inspire
> Her burning faculties, and with the wings
> Of thy unsphered flame visit'st the springs
> Of spirits immortal! Now (as swift as Time
> Doth follow Motion) find the eternal clime
> Of his free soul, whose living subject stood
> Up to the chin in the Pierian flood,
> And drunk to me half this Musaean story.

(Compare the description of Harriot "crowned with
heaven's inward brightness".)

The unsphered flame, beyond time and space, is
contrasted with the spheres of Time and Motion, the
Heraclitean flux. And Chapman's relation to Marlowe
is fairly described by these lines: for though the
influence is so obvious that everyone comments on it,
yet it is not to be traced to any common habits, or
direct borrowing. Chapman will occasionally "con-
vey" a line, as when he describes Julia:

> He saw the extraction of all fairest dames,
> The fair of beauty, as whole countries come
> And show their riches in a little room;
> > (*Ovid's Banquet of Sense*, ll. 318–20;
> > cf. *The Jew of Malta*, i. i. 37)

147

or Beauty:

> See where she issues in her beauty's pomp,
> As Flora to salute the morning sun;
> Who when she shakes her tresses in the air,
> Rains on the earth dissolved pearl in showers,
> Which with his beams the sun exhales to heaven;
> > (*England's Parnassus: Poems*, p. 429;
> > cf. *Tamburlaine, Part I*, 5. 2. 77–80)

or the horses of the sun:

> As when the fiery coursers of the sun
> Up to the palace of the morning run,
> And from their nostrils blow the spiteful day.
> > (*Hymnus in Cynthiam*, ll. 205–7;
> > cf. *Tamburlaine, Part II*, 4. 3. 7–9.)

But Chapman was incapable of imitating Marlowe on a large scale, and his continuation of *Hero and Leander* is a complete failure as a continuation, though as a separate poem it is not bad. Katherine Mansfield once accused Chapman of "putting that divine poem into a blouse and skirt", but the artificiality is quite intentional. Though he invokes Marlowe, Chapman from the beginning repudiates his methods: and it is plain that he meant his part to contrast with Marlowe's rather as *The Rape of Lucrece* contrasts with *Venus and Adonis*. What Chapman is trying to do is suggested by the simile with which he equates Hero's state of mind after Leander has left her with the state of the town after "Cadiz Action":

# CHAPMAN

Sweet Hero left upon her bed alone,
Her maidenhead, her vows, Leander gone,
And nothing with her but a violent crew
Of newcome thoughts that yet she never knew,
Even to herself a stranger, was much like
Th'Iberian city that war's hand did strike
By English force in princely Essex' guide
When Peace assured her towers had fortified,
And golden-fingered India had bestowed
Such wealth on her that strength and empire
    flowed
Into her turrets, and her virgin waist
The wealthy girdle of the sea embraced....

> (Third Sestiad, ll. 219 ff.)

Hero's perplexed state is analysed at great length, as she sits muffled in black "like a scorchèd statue made a coal". The visions which appear to Leander and Hero, the lengthy description of Hero's scarf, the wedding, and the story of Hymen are all meant to enforce Chapman's argument, which is, oddly enough, the realistic one of the complexity and self-deception of Hero's state of mind; the betrayal of her office left her hopelessly divided in loyalties, for even love cannot absorb the whole self; it is idolatry to think so.

What her heart
Did greatest hold in her self greatest part
That she did make her god.

> (Third Sestiad, ll. 184–6.)

# CHAPMAN

Chapman's mistake was to attempt to embody this in the sensuous-symbolic machinery of visions and sacrifices, instead of giving it directly; that is, analytically, or dramatically.

He needed less mythology and more logic. His energy was not harnessed or directed: it was a blind force, and all the apparatus which he constructed to shape it failed. He is usually considered to be primarily an epic poet and to have written plays only from necessity: but his plays are in fact his most successful writings, because in the scheme of his tragedies[15] and the intrigues of comedy he could canalize the ingenuity which otherwise spent itself in devising analogies and conceits.

The general effect of the School of Night upon him does not seem to have been a happy one. Chapman had not the type of mind to enter into its best work, and he could not have found it easy to work with a group at all. But some of the individual members were evidently his closest friends. Roydon, Harriot and Marlowe between them formed his mind and his style; and it was probably due in part to their friendship that he developed so rapidly from Henslowe's hack poet of the early nineties to the author of *Bussy D'Ambois*.

# VII

## SHAKESPEARE, THE SCHOOL, AND NASHE

O sacred eyes! the springs of living light,
The earthly heavens where angel joyes do dwell,...
Sweet volumes, stored with learning fit for saints,
When blissful quires imparadise their minds;
Wherein eternal studie never faints,
Still finding all, yet seeking all it finds:
How endless is your labyrinthe of bliss,
Where to be lost the sweetest finding is!

ROBERT SOUTHWELL, *St Peter's Complaint.*

*Love's Labour's Lost* was among other things Shakespeare's account of the School of Night. That is not all that goes to it, even in the way of topical allusion, as Miss Yates' study has shown: and the topical allusion furnishes only a side-line in the play. It may be questioned if anything comes out of Shakespeare's mind recognizably akin to what it was on going in: but assuming that it did, *Love's Labour's Lost* may be partly accounted for as follows.

Ralegh, having been banished from Court, betook himself to study, and even protested that a hermit's life was the life he had always wanted. From any other courtier this would have been a clear case of sour grapes: it probably was from him. Moreover, having been banished for a love affair, he allowed Chapman to write against the pleasure of love-making with great vehemence; and all his following made a parade of study, particularly of astronomy and philosophy.

The situation tempted mockery. Shakespeare drew a very realistic picture of the Court: its games, its sets of wits, its love-tokens and masquing and sonnets and riddles, its submerged money matters and jealous competitions coming to the surface now and then and giving a jar to the gaiety. Being Shakespeare, he also added a closing scene which covers the courtly games and the courtly mode with two narrow words "hic jacet".

Shakespeare was not making a jibe but a joke: he did not aim the whole play at the school, but brought in some hits 'and hints by the way. The personal caricature was used for the low comedy: Ferdinand and his lords, however like their creeds to Ralegh's, represent the opposite party, from the moment the princess arrives. But there is a tall and fantastic traveller, a knight, who spends his time writing poetry and penning long letters to his sovereign telling of imaginary plots, who rewrites old ballads, who addresses his servant with a West Country "Chirrah"[1] and who writes love-letters in Ercles' vein.

Armado fits Ralegh perfectly. The fact that he is a Spaniard is such an insult to one of the sea-dogs that it also serves as positive evidence. The king gives his character at length: he is a literary man, an orator and a writer:

> A man in *all the world's new fashions planted*
> That hath a mint of phrases in his brain.
> One whom the music of his own vain tongue
> Doth ravish like enchanting harmony....
> How you delight, my lords, I know not, I,
> But I protest *I love to hear him lie.*
>
> (1. 1. 164 ff.)

The dandy and planter of Virginia, spinner of travellers' tales, appears at once in "fashion's own knight". Armado's literary interests distinguish him

154

from the simple braggart-like Bobadil: but they are not detachable from that "humour", for his plausible tongue and complimentary flourishes are the weapons of his pride. He is "the magnificent Armado", upon whose shoulder the king leans, dallying with his mustachio; but to pluck his plumes he is compared to "the fantastical Monarcho", a crazy Italian megalomaniac who haunted the Court in the eighties, and of whom the poet Churchyard wrote an account.

In his letter to the king, Armado announces himself, "besieged with sable-coloured melancholy". Soon he appears, still melancholy. We learn that he is in his "old time", a "tough senior" (Ralegh was forty-one, about fifteen years older than Essex. His melancholy was more than a fashion: but he may have helped to set a fashion for it. At all events, Essex' party would treat it as affectation.) The knight is "in love",[2] and with a base wench: as a soldier he resents his captivity, but as a man he submits and desires the comfort of precedents, Hercules and Samson. Armado's military pretensions are very much stressed here, and in all the other scenes; there was nothing of which Essex was so jealous, and later he attempted to hang Ralegh for stealing a successful advance on him during the Islands Voyage.

It is also made plain that Armado is uncomfortably short of money. Costard only gets a three-farthing tip and the knight goes "woolward for penance". Throughout 1592–3 Ralegh was protesting with vigour (and justice) that the queen had taken all the profits of the *Madre de Dios* for herself and her favourites: he had barely recovered his outlay. He wrote desperate letters to her and to Burghley on this subject.

Armado decides to have *King Cophetua and the Beggar-Maid* refashioned for his turn. (*Walsingham* is quoted in *Hamlet*.) The next time he appears he is still as melancholy as ever: and his page sings an Irish song. It is in this scene also that he and Moth recite the mysterious rhyme

> The Fox, the Ape and the Humble Bee
> Were still at odds, being but three....
> Until the Goose came out of door
> Staying the odds by adding four.

All three animals give aspects of Ralegh: the Fox his Machiavellianism[3], the Ape court flattery, the Humble Bee court amours. Riddles of three persons in one are common enough. *At odds* is a codpiece joke: *goose* was slang for prostitute. (For the Humble Bee and the last two items see *Troilus and Cressida*, 4. 5. 41–4, 5. 10. 42 ff.) The riddle is thus an indecent statement of the intrigue between Ralegh and Mistress Throckmorton, which stopped all three of his activities.

Holofernes and Nathaniel describe Armado's person as well as his manner: "his humour is lofty, his discourse peremptory, his tongue filed, his eye ambitious, his gate majestical, and his general behaviour vain, ridiculous and thrasonical". But when Armado invites Holofernes to "be singled from the barbarous" with him, to arrange some theatricals, the pedant is flattered enough to appropriate all the best parts. And indeed Armado calculates nicely between imposing reminiscence and buttering of the schoolmaster.

In the show Armado takes the part of Hector of Troy, so that he wears very imposing armour when Costard rushes in with the news that Jaquenetta is "two months upon her way", popularly supposed to be the same predicament (though there is no evidence for it) which landed Ralegh in the Tower. But Armado discreetly arranges matters so that he does not have to fight.[4] Finally he chooses to retire from court to the country with his wench and hold the plough for her love three years. Ralegh held it for five.

There can be little question of Armado, "a soldier, a man of travel, that hath seen the world". His literary style may seem too conceited to be even a parody of Ralegh's: but it probably does represent fairly well his own early manner of writing: the manner of "Your face, your tongue, your wit", "Fain would I, but I dare not" and "No pleasure without some

Pain". One might not unfairly compare a stanza of
the first of these—

> Your face, your tongue, your wit
> So fine, so sweet, so sharp,
> First bent, then drew, so hit
> Mine eye, mine eare, my heart—

with Armado's exposition of *King Cophetua*:

He came, saw and overcame; he came, one; saw,
two; overcame, three. Who came? the king; Why did
he come? to see; Why did he see? to overcome; To
whom came he? to the beggar; What saw he? the
beggar; Who overcame he? the beggar. The conclusion is victory; On whose side? the king's: The captive
is enrich'd; On whose side? the beggar's: The catastrophe is a nuptial: On whose side? the king's?—
no, on both in one, or one in both.

And the delicious hauteur of his poem is typically
Ralegh's:

> Thus dost thou hear the Nemean lion roar
> 'Gainst thee, thou lamb, that standest as his prey:
> Submissive fall his princely feet before,
> And he from forage will incline to play.
> But if thou strive, poor soul, what art thou then?
> Food for his rage, repasture for his den.

Armado is the only true victim of the "little
academe's" monastic rule. The king and his lords are
forsworn more lightly; and besides "Jack has not Jill".

They are discomfited, like the wooers in *Willobie his Avisa*. But Armado is more of a character than anyone (except Berowne, who stands between Mercutio and Benedick, and has the graces and gracelessness of both). The only thing he lacks is a silver tobacco pipe to give action in his melancholy musings.

Ralegh's marriage must have seemed to Essex as providential as Berowne's collapse to his wit-riddled companion. For only in 1590, Essex had married Walsingham's daughter Frances, widow of Philip Sidney. This was so much more heinous than his habit of getting the maids of honour with child that he concealed it as long as he could: and Elizabeth, when it finally came out, banished him the Court for a time. Lady Sidney, she considered, had been his social inferior: Essex had polluted his blood. The countess lived "very retired in her mother's house", and was never readmitted to Court. How Ralegh's wit was barbed on this occasion may easily be conjectured.

Consequently when Ralegh was discovered in an even more invidious situation, Essex would have the last laugh. This is one more reason for identifying Ferdinand and his companions with Essex, and keeping Ralegh's part to Armado: and it underlines the very positive tone of triumph and achievement that accompanies the breaking of the vow.

The Nine Worthies have other of "the Lord's

tokens" on them than this. They all show a taste for scholastic methods of argument, particularly of course when the subject is Love (1. 1. 217 ff., 1. 2. 160 ff., 1. 4. 34 ff., 4. 3. 1 ff.), and an inability for the simplest mathematics (1. 2. 40–53, 3. 1. 143–7, 5. 2. 491–6, 5. 2. 530–9). Dull asks a riddle about Dictynna, "a title to Luna, to Phebe, to the Moon", and there are a surprising number of references to astronomy, though they belong quite as much to the noblemen as to the low comedy. The insistence on the power of women's eyes, on which several critics have commented, becomes more pointed if it is remembered at what length Chapman contemns the bodily eyesight as the origins of all temptations and sins (*Hymnus in Noctem*, ll. 362–5).[5] Miss Yates has worked out the antithesis between eyes and stars as symbols of active and contemplative living, and has connected it with the fortunes of Essex' two sisters, "Stella", and the Countess of Northumberland. The former was the cause of an old dispute between Sidney and the astronomer Giordano Bruno on the merits of love and learning: the Countess of Northumberland provoked the letter of Essex and the poem of Ralegh which I have discussed in chapter II, and her unhappy marriage to Ralegh's friend aggravated the feud between the two circles. (See *A Study of Love's Labour's Lost*, chapters VI and VII.)

160

Miss Yates has worked out many references in the farcical sub-plot of the play, some to people unconnected with the School of Night, such as John Florio, tutor to the Earl of Southampton, and as she believes, the subject of caricature in Holofernes. I think there might possibly be a reflection upon Harriot, who was well known to be the master conjuror of the school, and to educate many noble youths. The friendliness of Armado towards him ("Arts-man, perambulate. We will be singled from the barbarous...") also suggests Harriot.

But the play is on the whole more concerned with theories of living than with personalities: the satire is not sustained and consistent. The convenient masks of the *Commedia dell' Arte*, Braggart, Pedant and Zany, gave a stiff framework into which many different hits could be worked without interference with each other. Shakespeare's real interest was in the general theme of active *versus* contemplative living. That he managed to deal with it without much theorizing is a proof of how thoroughly his methods embodied his convictions. He does not preach against the preachers, and if the number of references to the Anglican liturgy and the Bishops' Bible which Mr Richmond Noble has detected in the play suggest that Shakespeare had been affected by the school's reputation for atheism, they are sufficiently diffused and oblique to show that he was not making an issue of it in his poetry.

Shakespeare begins with the much safer and subtler method of parodying the other party's taste for theory, in particular the writing of Chapman. For example, in their opening speeches the king and his followers give a statement of their resolve in a style which recalls Chapman's symbolism of conflict:

> Therefore, brave conquerors! for so you are
> That war against your own affections,
> And the huge army of the world's desires,—
> Our late edict shall strongly stand in force.

And later there is a reminiscence of his gnomic style, with its condensed analogies:

> The mind shall banquet, though the body pine:
> Fat paunches have lean pates: and dainty bits
> Make rich the ribs, but bankerout the wits;

or of his magniloquence:

> The grosser manner of these world's delights
> He throws upon the gross world's baser slaves:
> To love, to wealth, to pomp, I pine and die:
> With all these living in philosophy.[6]

And against them he sets Berowne's doctrine that it is presumptuous to think one can learn as well by effort as by allowing the world to do the teaching, and that learning is only of use to lead to richer daily living.

> Study is like the heaven's glorious sun,
> That will not be deep-search'd with saucy looks;
> Small have continual plodders ever won,
> Save base authority from others' books.
> These earthly godfathers of heaven's lights
> That give a name to every fixed star,
> Have no more profit of their shining nights,
> Than those that walk, and wot not what they are.

Both, if Shakespeare had known, were very close to the doctrines of Chapman himself. As he had put it in an epigram:

> Learning the art is of good life: they, then,
> That lead not good lives, are not learned men,

and Ralegh had pointed out that the cheese-wife and the philosopher were in the same position when it came to a final definition of cheese-making.

Both this scene and the corresponding one in which the lords discover their perjury (4. 2) appear from the bibliographical evidence to be practically untouched by revision.[7] When all have confessed, and Berowne bursts into praise of his dark lady, heavenly Rosaline, there is an unequivocal reference to Ralegh's school:

> No face is fair that is not full as black

## SHAKESPEARE,

Berowne exclaims, and the king replies

> O paradox! Black is the badge of hell,
> The hue of dungeons and the School of Night.

Ralegh's swarthy colouring, Ralegh's atheism, his recent imprisonment and his coterie are all neatly hit off in the two lines. The mocking of the school goes on in references to colliers and chimney-sweeps and a luridly indecent adaptation of an image from the *Hymnus in Cynthiam*[8] till Berowne is asked to justify them all: "some salve for perjury". He sets off with mock-philosophic reasons, the kind of argument the School of Night might have used to justify Ralegh:

> Why, universal plodding prisons up
> The nimble spirits in the arteries:...
> Learning is but an adjunct to ourself,
> And where we are, our learning likewise is.
> Then, when ourselves we see in ladies' eyes,
> Do we not likewise see our learning there?

But he soon soars off from parody to his former arguments, and with an attack on "leaden contemplation" he sings the active life in Marlovian verse:

> Other slow arts entirely keep the brain;
> And therefore finding barren practisers,
> Scarce show a harvest of their heavy toil:
> But love, first learned in a lady's eyes,
> Lives not alone immured in the brain;

But with the motion of all elements,
Courses as swift as thought in every power,
And gives to every power a double power,
Above their functions and their offices.
It adds a precious seeing to the eye:
A lover's eyes will gaze an eagle blind:
A lover's ear will hear the lowest sound,
When the suspicious head of theft is stopp'd;
Love's feeling is more soft, and sensible,
Than are the tender horns of cockled snails,
Love's tongue proves dainty Bacchus gross in taste:
For valour, is not love a Hercules,
Still climbing trees in the Hesperides?
Subtle as sphinx, as sweet and musical
As bright Apollo's lute, strung with his hair;
And, when love speaks, the voice of all the gods
Makes heaven drowsy with the harmony.
Never durst poet touch a pen to write,
Unless his ink were temper'd with love's sighs;
O, then his lines would ravish savage ears
And plant in tyrants mild humility.
From women's eyes this doctrine I derive:
They sparkle still the right Promethean fire;
They are the books, the arts, the academes
That show, contain, and nourish all the world.

(4. 3. 321–50.)

Chapman has his answer: and part of it comes from
*Tamburlaine*, part from *Hero and Leander*.[9]

Shakespeare does not refute, he counters; or as
Goldsmith would have said, knocks Chapman down

with the butt of his pistol. Instead of suppressing the senses with the physical world of the "elements" and their "motion", he invokes love to give them a double power. Instead of escaping from the flux, he immerses in it: the world is to be "nourished" by the Art of Love, and "barren practisers" are rejected because their "slow arts" are unable to enrich daily living.

It is not a case which Shakespeare presents, but an appeal. The glow and blaze of the poetry would confute Chapman as poet, if one poet could "confute" another: but the very conception is irrelevant to the kind of statement which poetry conveys. The "confuting" is not a matter only of the greater richness and concreteness of his language, though it is partly that: it is the difference between

> Subtle as Sphinx; as sweet and musical
> As bright Apollo's lute, strung with his hair,
> And when Love speaks, the voice of all the Gods
> Makes Heaven drowsy with the harmony!

and

> He still'd
> All sounds in air and left so free my ears
> As I might hear the music of the spheres,
> And all the angels singing out of heaven.

Shakespeare's tone is fuller because it is not based on exclusions. He can catch up myth, and the physical implication of a word like "drowsy" and "strung" with the modulations of his easy sinuous movement, and yet produce a tone as heavenly clear as Chapman's and far mellower. In short, Shakespeare, like Marlowe, was poet enough to have it both ways: and Chapman must come limping after. Chapman is writing of a very special state of mind attained by labour, the calm at the centre of the whirlpool; Shakespeare of "an enchanting and attainable perfection of actuality".[10]

There was not a great deal to be done by publishing *Ovid's Banquet of Sense* now, and trying to prove that contemplation produced all the delights of the senses in a purified form; and if Shakespeare's last few lines have a fling at Chapman's mysticism, it is more in exultation than in parody. Shakespeare did not belittle what he mocked: he simply caught it up and kindled such a blaze of poetry on it that the original faded away, "an attending star, scarce seen a light".

All the dozens of references to logic and mathematics and astronomy and pedantic Latinisms are not so many separate and spiteful little darts: they function apart from that purpose. Shakespeare, having decided what he was going to make fun of, could go ahead without having to think all the time of that: on the contrary, he wrote a play close-packed enough to be watered down into two or three, and found his

"facetious grace in writing" had not needed calculation. Half the pleasure of discovering the allusions lies
in finding how perfectly they are digested, and with
what ease Shakespeare contrived to do half-a-dozen
things at once. The references are just obvious enough
to be recognizable where we have the clues, or to
produce a slight consciousness of secondary intentions
where we have not.[11] But compared with, say, *The
Poetaster*, how masterly it includes both the wood and
the trees!

The school's retort to *Love's Labour's Lost* was
*Willobie His Avisa*, a narrative which tells how different
gentlemen make verbal assaults upon the chastity of
Avisa, wife of an innkeeper, and all are gloriously
repulsed. This harmless little book went into a second
edition rapidly and was then ordered to be burnt along
with such scandalous pamphlets as those of the Mar-
prelates. Its preface is written in a very sly manner,
hinting that the story may be true, that it must be
true, but that the truth cannot be discovered. Dr G. B.
Harrison has convincingly identified the scene of this
story as the George Inn, Cerne Abbas; and of the
identity of the last suitor at least there has been generally little conjecture. He is accepted as Southampton.

H. W... bewrayeth the secret of his disease unto
his familiar friend W. S., who not long before had
tryed the courtesy of the like passion, and was now

newly recovered of the like infection... and in viewing afar off the course of this loving Comedy, he determined to see whether it would sort to a happier end for this new actor, than it did for the old player.

W. S. meets his friend in a lively vein:

> Well met, friend Harry, what's the cause
> You look so pale with Lented cheeks?
> Your wanny face and sharpened nose
> Show plain your mind some thing mislikes.

When he has heard of H. W.'s passion for Avisa, he cheers the forlorn lover briskly with a tag from his plays:

> She is no Saynt, she is no Nonne,
> I think in tyme she may be wonne.[12]

But H. W. speeds no better than any of his predecessors, the Nobleman, the Cavaliero, the Frenchman, D. B., or the German Didymus Harco. He woos Avisa through dozens of cantoes, with arguments, with letters, with offers of wealth: but the immovable landlady repulses him as steadily, till in despair he goes away, no one knows where.

The most striking fact about *Willobie His Avisa* is its disjointedness. The introduction is written by one Hadrian Dorrell, an Oxford scholar, who discovered the poems among the papers of his friend Henry Willobie (a recognized "device" to cover publication). There are also introductory verses by "Abel

Emmet" and another friend. Willobie is evidently meant to have written the main poem, but at the end he speaks of himself in the third person. Then there is the question of the other wooers' identity: and the book concludes with songs, several written by Willobie, one to the tune of "Fortune", one in lumbering poulter's measure. The style of the main poem is very uneven: in the first two encounters of Avisa it is quite polished and brisk, but it tails off badly.

All this, I think, suggests collaboration: the various members of the school each added a portion to the riposte. The fact that the upshot of this love-story is the same as that in *Love's Labour's Lost* should not escape attention, even if an innkeeper's wife has replaced the Princess of France. The narrative in the poem is reduced to a minimum, and the main body of it consists of long speeches from Avisa and her wooer: in other words, a continued debate upon the subject of Berowne's speech. Avisa supports her case with liberal quotations from the Scriptures: but she also glances at the riddles of Mr W. S. in vigorous terms:

> Methinks I see a sober Fox,
> Stands preaching to the gagling Geese:
> And showe them out a painted box
> And bid them all beware of cheese:
> Your painted box and godly preach
> I see doth hold a boxly reach....

# THE SCHOOL, AND NASHE

It's ill to halt before the lame
Or watch the bird that cannot sleepe,
Your new found tricks are out of frame;
The Fox will laugh when Asses weepe:
Sweare what you list, say what you will,
Before you spake, I knew your skill.

The aim of the school seems to have been to parody Shakespeare's phrases directly, as he had parodied them, and to show that they could be even more colloquial and mock-magniloquent if need be. The "Author's Conclusion" refers to Avisa as "A Lambe amid the Lion's paws" in palpable imitation of Armado's sonnet and goes on to say

While hand can write, while wit devise,
While tongue is free to make report,
Thy vertue shall be had in prise....

Devise wit, write pen, for I am for whole volumes in folio! (*Love's Labour's Lost*, 1. 2. 176–7.)

But *Willobie His Avisa* is the complement to *Love's Labour's Lost* in more senses than one. The writers were absorbed in making their hits, and, when the key to the situation is lost, their little poem becomes quite unintelligible. In this, and many other ways, the book resembles Robert Chester's compilation, *Love's Martyr*, for which Shakespeare wrote.

In *Love's Labour's Lost* another writer is drawn into Armado's circle. Almost certainly his page, Moth,

the "tender juvenal", has some features in common
with Thomas Nashe.[13] Moth is not a very respectful
follower: his wit cuts both ways, but it is exercised as
often on behalf of Armado as against him. There is
no evidence to connect Thomas Nashe with Ralegh,
but in October 1594 he published a pamphlet, *The
Terrors of the Night*, jestingly dedicated to Elizabeth
Carey, the young daughter of Ralegh's friend and
co-member of the school, Sir George Carey, the "skill-
embracing Heir of Hunsdon", Marshal of the Household and Governor of the Isle of Wight. Nashe had
been staying in the island during the winter of 1592–3,
and it was probably in that year he wrote the pamphlet. He says to Mistress Carey that she knows "from
whose motive imposition it first proceeded as also
what strange sodaine cause necessarily produced that
motion". But the only present cause which appears
is to illustrate a story of the strange dreams of a certain
gentleman living "not three score miles from London".

The pamphlet is written in very high spirits, even
for Nashe: his mood is one of mock-horror, and
extreme credulity. He imagines devils everywhere.

It is impossible the gunnes should go off as they do
if there were not a spirit, either in the fire, or in the
powder.

Now for worms; what make a dog run mad, but a
worme in his tong? and what should that worme be

172

but a spirit? Is there anie reason such small vermine as they are, should devour such a vast thing as a shippe, or have the teeth to gnawe through yron and wood? No, no, they are spirits, or else it were incredible....

If the bubbels in streames were all searcht, I am persuaded they would be found to be little better.... Not so much as Tewkesburie mustard but hath a spirit in it, or els it would never bite so.

Nashe declaims at length upon the devilish nature of the Night and of its astronomy; "the devil is a special predominant Planet of the Night". He will not list the devil's names, lest men think he is about to conjure. But in support of the devils' fondness for the Night, Nashe quotes the poets ("which it cannot be but the divell hath read"). All this is delivered in measured and almost ecclesiastic gravity. It might equally well discomfit those who spread tales about the School of Night, and those members of it who took themselves too seriously. When Nashe comes to describe the Spirits of the Elements, he dwells at particular length upon the first, the Spirits of the Fire:

Or Poets, or boon companions they are, out of question....It is almost impossible for any to be incumbred with ill spirits who is continually conversant in the excellent restorative distillations of wit and of alcumie. Those that ravenously englut them-

173

selves with gross meates and respect not the quality but the quantity of what they eate, have no affinitie with these spirits of the fire.

This is consoling; but Nashe does not remain tractable. The next paragraph is mock-puritanical, and has more of a sting. Chapman's attack on the senses and his fury against the vulgar Mr W. S. are involved.

A man that will entertain them must not pollute his bodie with any gross carnall copulation or inordinate beastly desires, but love pure beauty, pure virtue, and not have his affections, linsey-wolsey, intermingled with lust and things worthy of liking. As for example, if he love good Poets he must not countenance Ballad makers. . . .

And he ends with a severe warning against the spirits of the fire who are

By nature, ambitious, haughty and proud

and

A humour of Monarchising and nothing els it is, which makes them affect rare quallified studies. Many Atheists are with these spirits inhabited.

This is half-faced praise: and the way in which Nashe goes on to give a rationalist explanation of dreams would have outraged Chapman, though it might have pleased Harriot. He then comes to the main purpose of his tract, the mysterious dream. It is prefaced by the remark that "In all points our brains are like the firmament, and exhale in everie respect the like grose mistempered vapors and meteors."

His story concerns a "wise, grave, sensible man" who the February before fell sick. He lived "in the Country some threescore myle off from London". In his sickness this gentleman was subject to remarkable visions: first he saw the devil fishing in his room, which was all hung with silken nets and silver hooks.

Next a company of lusty sailors came asking him to drink with them: "Fellowes they were that had good big pop mouths to cry Port a helme Saint George and knew as well as the best what belongs to halings of bolings yare and falling on the starboord buttocke" (Avisa, it will be rembered, lived at the George Inn, "where captains cry Victorious land to conquering rage").

After the sailors, a pageant of stately devils brought in chests of treasure, and Lucifer himself came in to tempt the gentleman: but the gentleman gave him his answer.

Then, "for the third pageant", he saw a troop of virgins, stark naked, whose hair hung in amber trammels, and whose breath "more perfumed the aire than Ordinance would, that is charged with Amomum, Muske, Civit and Ambergreece". When the gentleman resisted their blandishments, "for the fourth act" he was assailed by an assembly of Matrons "much like the Virgins of Marie Magdalen's order in Rome". These offered to pray for him: and for half an hour he and they joined prayers most devoutly; at the end of which

Rising up agayne on the right hand of his bed, there appeared a cleare light, and with that he might perceive a naked slender foote offering to steale betwixte the sheets in to him.

At this point he was rescued by a quintessence, sent him from "a Knight of great honour thereabouts", which dispelled the vision. Unfortunately he soon grew worse again, and two days later he died.

Now the vision, according to Nashe, is the sole reason of his writing the pamphlet. And if there are any doubts of "this incredible Narration" he will resolve them.

First the house where this Gentleman dwelt, stood in a low Marishe ground, almost as rotten a clymate as the Low Countreyes: where their mystie ayre is as thick as mould butter and the deaw lies like frothie balme upon the ground. It was noted over and beside to have been an unluckie house to all his predecessors, situate in a quarter not altogether exempt from witches.

# THE SCHOOL, AND NASHE

There is one member of the School of Night who was notoriously "wise, grave and sensible" and yet spoke of seeing visions. That was Chapman, and his home was about 30 miles from London, in the fen country, at Hitchin. Moreover, in April 1593 there had been a great witch-scandal, that of the "Witches of Warboys", in the neighbouring county of Huntingdon. He had published his visionary Σκιὰ νυκτὸς and was just about to publish his *Ovid's Banquet of Sense*, a tempting subject for ribaldry. This poem is divided into five sections, corresponding to the five senses: the gentleman's "vision" is divided into five acts (for Nashe evidently does not count the first, as it was not a temptation). The poem describes how Ovid surprises Julia bathing, and feasts each of his five senses in turn, but all, according to Chapman, in the most spiritual fashion; while the lady holds a philosophic discourse with him, dressed in a tinsel mantle. It is possible that Nashe saw it in MS.

Chapman had prefixed to the poem one of his most defiant prefaces. There is no question that in his stubborn, courageous way he was trying to put the case for what a psychologist would now call Sublimation.[14] But it would have taken another mystic, a Crashaw or a Blake, to read his eroticism without misinterpretation. Nashe certainly could not; the vision shows plainly enough what he made of it. He underlined his present triumph by parodying Chapman's motto for his work: "Post Tenebras Dies".

His rationalist interpretation of dreams (as confused recollection of mundane events) makes it plain that if Chapman had a vision of a naked woman, he ought to have written something like the second Sestiad of *Hero and Leander*. Nashe would have been very surprised if he could have foreseen what Chapman would do when he continued that work of "the divine Musaeus, and a diviner Muse than he, Kit Marlowe".

Nashe hunted with the pack. The School of Night could not hope to escape calumny: and Chapman was always in special danger of ridicule. Ralegh stimulated Marlowe; and Chapman was Marlowe's pupil. Together they laid the foundations for the metaphysical poets who were to be among the most powerful poetic forces of the new century.

# NOTES

References are to the following editions:

John Aubrey. *Brief Lives*, ed. Andrew Clark. (Oxford, 1890.)

George Chapman. *Works*, ed. A. Swinburne. (Chatto and Windus, 1875.)

—— *Tragedies and Comedies*, ed. T. M. Parrott. (Routledge, London, 1910–13.)

Christopher Marlowe. *Works*, ed. R. H. Case. (Methuen, London, 1929–34.)

Thomas Nashe. *Works*, ed. R. B. McKerrow. (A. H. Bullen, London, 1904.)

Sir Walter Ralegh. *Works*, ed. Oldys and Birch. (Oxford, 1829.)

—— *Poems*, ed. Agnes M. C. Latham. (Constable, London, 1929.)

William Shakespeare. *Works*. Globe edition. (Macmillan, London, 1921.)

—— *Love's Labour's Lost*, ed. Quiller-Couch and Dover Wilson. (Cambridge New Shakespeare, 1923.)

Edmund Spenser. *Works*. Globe edition. (Macmillan, London, 1924.)

*Willobie His Avisa*, ed. G. B. Harrison. (Bodley Head Quartos, 1926.)

Antony à Wood. *Athenae Oxonienses*. (London, 1691.)

### CHAPTER I

1. Janet Spens, *The Faerie Queene*, chapter 1.

2. *Love's Labour's Lost*, 4. 3. 214.

3. Henry Stevens of Vermont, *Thomas Harriot and his Associates*. (Privately printed, 1900.)

# NOTES

4. *Responsio ad Elizabethae Edictum.*

5. Thomas Kyd, Letter to Sir John Puckering. Reprinted by F. S. Boas, in *Marlowe and his Circle* (1929).

6. Samuel Tannenbaum, *The Assassination of Christopher Marlowe* (1928).

7. Thomas Kyd, Letter to Sir John Puckering.

8. Richard Baines, A Note...of the most horrible blasphemies uttered by Christofer Marley. Quoted by F. S. Boas, *op. cit.*

9. Walter Ralegh, *The Sceptic* (*Works*, vol. VIII, p. 554).

10. Aubrey, *Brief Lives*, vol. II, p. 188.

### CHAPTER II

1. Ralegh had provoked it (*Poems*, p. 69).

2. Aubrey, *Brief Lives*, vol. II, p. 184.

3. George Puttenham, *The Art of Poesy* (1589).

4. Lyly's *Endimion* appeared in 1585.

5. Prof. J. E. Neale, *Queen Elizabeth*, p. 214.

6. Ralph M. Sargent, *At the Court of Queen Elizabeth*, pp. 22–3.

7. Walter Ralegh, *Apology* (*Works*, vol. VIII, pp. 494–5).

8. Walter Ralegh, Epistle Dedicatory to *The Discovery of Guiana* (*Works*, vol. VIII, p. 381).

9. Walter Ralegh, Preface to *The History of the World* (*Works*, vol. II, p. xlv).

10. Walter Ralegh, *Works*, vol. VIII, p. 427.

11. Walter Ralegh, *Works*, vol. VIII, p. 638.

# NOTES

## CHAPTER III

1. Walter Ralegh, *A Treatise of the Soul* (*Works*, vol. VIII, p. 574).

2. Cf. William Warner, *Albion's England*, Book XIII, chap. LXXVIII.

> Omit we operation with thy body's action, and
> Thy soul infused throughout the whole, one of our
>   powerful band,
> And to thy understanding soul (thy soul's soul) let
>   us come.

3. Sir Edmund Chambers, "The Disenchantment of the Elizabethans", in *Sir Thomas Wyatt and some Collected Studies*, p. 199.

4. Infra-red and ultra-violet rays, for instance.

5. Walter Ralegh, *Works*, vol. II, p. xliii. Cf. "What is our life? a play of passion" (*Poems*, p. 48).

6. Cf. William Warner, *Albion's England*, Book XIII, chap. LXXVIII.

> God's Nature past all kenning of man's Science quite
>   extends,
> Nor more from man of science than those senses had,
>   descends.

7. Francis Bacon, *De Augmentis Scientiae* (Bohn), Book IX, pp. 368 ff. Quoted by Basil Willey, *The Seventeenth Century Background* (1933), p. 28.

8. Basil Willey, *op. cit.* p. 29.

9. Letter to his brothers, December 1817.

10. Walter Ralegh, Preface to *The History of the World* (*Works*, vol. II, p. xxxi).

# NOTES

11. William Warner, *Albion's England,* Book XIII, chap. LXXIX.

12. This fits particularly well with Spenser and the Cabbala. See Prof. Denis Saurat, *Literature and Occult Tradition* (1928), chap. v.

13. T. S. Eliot, "Shakespeare and the Stoicism of Seneca" in *Selected Essays* (1932).

14. Heraclitus, Fragment 20 (ed. Bywater). Augustine, *Civ. Dei.* VIII, 5.

15. Cicero, *Nat. Deor.* III, 14, 36.

16. Cicero (quoting Zeno), *Ac.* I, 11, 39.

17. Seneca, *Ep. Mor.* 94, 56. Cf. *Hymnus in Noctem,* ll. 123–30.

18. Heraclitus, Fragment 4. Seneca, *Ep. Mor.* 65, 16; 92, 93. Cf. *Hymnus in Noctem,* ll. 363–9; *Hymnus in Cynthiam,* ll. 216–20.

19. Plato, *Crat.* 402.

20. R. Adamson, *Greek Philosophy before Plato,* p. 44.

21. "One man is to me as a thousand, if he be the best." Heraclitus, Fragment 117.

22. Elizabeth Holmes, *Henry Vaughan and the Hermetic Philosophy,* p. 28.

23. I am indebted for these references to C. A. Bennett, *A Philosophical Study of Mysticism* (Yale), pp. 46–7.

24. For the marriage of the sun god and the moon goddess, see A. B. Cook, *Zeus,* I, pp. 521 ff.

25. Dionysius speaks of "the sovereign shining darkness of wisest silence" of "making the sovereign clearest sovereignly for to shine privily in the darkest: and the

182

# NOTES

which is in a manner that is always invisible and un-gropable, sovereignly fulfilling with full fair clarities all those souls that be not having eyes of mind".

26. *Ralegh's Staattheoretische Schriften: die Einführung des Machiavellismus in England*. Von Nadja Kempner (Leipzig, 1928).

## CHAPTER IV

1. S. T. Coleridge, *Biographia Literaria*, chap. XVI.

2. Probably written in the same year (1593).

3. T. S. Eliot, "Dante", *Selected Essays*, p. 259.

4. In Robert Bridges' sense of the word (i.e. as used in the phrase "in keeping with").

5. Matthew Arnold, *Dover Beach*.

6. E.g. "A Report of the truth of the late fight about the Azores", where personal feeling for his cousin Grenville would have been out of place.

## CHAPTER V

1. T. S. Eliot, "Shakespeare and the Stoicism of Seneca", *Selected Essays*, p. 133.

2. See chap. I, p. 17.

3. See chap. III, p. 62.

4. See chap. III, p. 66.

5. See chap. III, p. 65; chap. IV, p. 96.

6. Walter Ralegh, *A Treatise of the Soul* (*Works*, vol. VIII, p. 582).

7. Chapman calls Cynthia "Nature's bright eyesight and the Night's fair soul".

# NOTES

8. See chap. III, p. 71.

9. Part I, 1. 2. 44, 139–40, 181; 4. 3. 7–10, 22. Part II, 4. 3. 116.

10. Part I, 1. 2. 37–45; 3. 2. 19; 5. 2. 78–80, 452.

11. Part I, 5. 2. 88. Part II, 2. 4. 22; 3. 4. 50; 4. 3. 107, 128.

12. Cf. Trismegistus, *Poemander*, 14. "Nature showing the reflection of that most beautiful form (God's) in the water." Also Meister Eckhardt, trans. Evans, I, p. 143.

13. William Empson, *Seven Types of Ambiguity*, pp. 41–2. He is referring to *Tamburlaine, Part I*, 2. 5. 50–4, and *Dr Faustus*, 1. 1. 122–34.

14. See F. S. Boas, introduction to *Dr Faustus*, p. 38.

15. Cf. Warner, "And fighteth as she would be foiled."

16. According to L. C. Martin, a favourite word of Marlowe's.

17. *Metaphysics*, III, iv.

## CHAPTER VI

1. *Hymnus in Cynthiam*, ll. 151–3.

2. See chap. VII, p. 164: cf. F. M. Yates, *A Study of Love's Labour's Lost*, chap. IV.

3. Janet Spens, "Chapman's Ethical Thought", *Essays and Studies of the English Association*, vol. XI.

4. *To Mr Harriots*, ll. 30–40.

5. *Ibid.* ll. 42–3.

6. Trismegistus, *Poemander*, 10. 8, remarks that when a soul is evil it descends the ladder of creation as far as the reptiles.

# NOTES

7. Εὐθυμία. The sub-title of *The Tears of Peace* is "Euthymia Raptus".

8. *To Mr Harriots* "this foul panther earth". Cf. the Calydonian boars and *Bussy D'Ambois*, 5. 1. 92–3. Mt. Cytheron symbolizes the bestial also in *Hymnus in Cynthiam*, l. 14.

9. W. B. Yeats, *Collected Works*, vol. VI, p. 100.

10. Trismegistus, *Poemander*, 4. 16, says we must hate our bodies if we would love ourselves.

11. The common apology, of course.

12. *The Revenge of Bussy D'Ambois*, 1. 1. 170: cf. the epigram *Of Learning*.

13. *Andromeda Liberata* [*Poems*, p. 187, l. 1]: cf. *Two Gentlemen of Verona*, 2. 3. 41.

14. *The Tears of Peace*, Inductio (*Poems*, p. 112).

15. For an analysis of *Bussy D'Ambois*, see the article by James Smith in *Scrutiny*, June 1935.

### CHAPTER VII

1. Not genuine West Country: the "ch", a survival of the personal pronoun "ich", produced such forms as "chill" for "I will" (see *King Lear*, 4. 6. 234–44). Ralegh "spake broad Devonshire to his dying day" (Aubrey, *Brief Lives*, vol. II, p. 182).

2. Cf. the comment of the Princess of France on Navarre and his followers,

> The blood of youth burns not with such desire
> As gravity's revolt to wantonness. (5. 2. 73–4.)

It was quite inapplicable to the case before her.

3. When Ralegh was to give evidence at Essex' trial, the prisoner called out "What boots it to swear the fox?" The name was presumably due to his Machiavellianism. Cf. the proverb on parchment, pens and wax: "the Calf, the Goose, the Bee, the world is ruled by these three".

4. Essex had challenged Ralegh in 1587: they had been separated by order of the Privy Council.

5. The keen interest of the Nine Worthies in the princess' hunting, and the sonnet of Holofernes in particular may glance at the hunt in the *Hymnus in Cynthiam*.

6. Cf. *Hymnus in Noctem*, ll. 328–40.

7. See the Cambridge New Shakespeare, p. 116.

8. *Love's Labour's Lost*, 4.3.274–7: cf. *Hymnus in Cynthiam*, ll. 268–70.

9. *Tamburlaine, Part I*, 5. 2. 116–19. *Hero and Leander*, Second Sestiad, ll. 297–300, 827–8.

10. J. Middleton Murry, *Countries of the Mind*, p. 2.

11. E.g. the number of references to Hercules, which are quite noticeable and cannot be explained unless it is a reflection on Warner's attachment to the demigod. He wrote a panegyric on the letter H.

12. Cf. *Titus Andronicus*, 2. 1. 82–4; *Richard III*, 1. 2. 228–9.

13. See the Cambridge *New Shakespeare*, pp. xx–xxiii: F. M. Yates, *op. cit.* chap. iii.

14. Cf. *Hymnus in Noctem*, ll. 332–49, which might be taken as a motto for *Ovid's Banquet of Sense*.

# INDEX

187

# INDEX

188

# INDEX

# INDEX